# Drawing
# Families
# Together

## One Meal at a Time

by
**Jill Kimball**

with
Neal Kimball,
Dr. Stacey Tantleff-Dunn
and
Dr. Michael E. Dunn

Special introduction by
former First Lady
**Barbara Bush**

Active Media Publishing, LLC
Orlando, Florida

# Let These Icons Be a Guide to You!

**TOGETHER**
These are activities you can try together as a family.

Illustrated points that could help your family.

**EXAMPLE**

**MEAL TIME**
These are tips, tools and techniques set around the dinner table.

Statistics or data that might surprise and enlighten you.

**FUN FACT**

**QUOTES**
Words of wisdom from outside sources.

Important tips for you to remember.

**REMEMBER**

**IDEA**
Great idea for you to try with your family.

Caution, this is very crucial information.

**WARNING**

---

**Drawing Families Together, One Meal at a Time**
Published by **Active Media Publishing, LLC.**          Compiled by Brian W. Kelly
In association with
Active Media Enterprises  *  255 South Orange Avenue, Suite 600  *  Orlando, Florida  32801
www.ActiveMediaPublishing.com

Library of Congress Cataloging-in-Publication Data

Drawing families together, one meal at a time / by Jill Kimball ... [et al.] ; special introduction by Barbara Bush.
   p. cm.
 ISBN 0-9745645-0-8 (pbk.)
 1.  Family--United States. 2.  Communication in the family--United States. 3.  Parenting--United States. 4.  Dinners and dining.  I. Kimball, Jill.

 HQ536.D74 2003
 306.85'0973--dc22

                    2003020348

# TABLE OF CONTENTS

## Chapter Six:
## Dynamics of Family Communication ................................ 79

## Chapter Seven:
## Battling the Influence of Pop Culture ............................. 101

## Chapter Eight:
## Family Issues and Roles ............................................................. 117

## Chapter Nine:
## School Issues ................................................................................. 131

## Chapter Thirteen:
## Drug Issues ................................................................................................ 217

## Chapter Fourteen:
## Family Stress Issues .................................................................................. 235

# INTRODUCTION

**From the Desk of Barbara Bush**

Dear Friends,

You could say my relationship with the Kimball family began in a rather inauspicious way. Several years ago their daughter Caitlin stood up at a town meeting in Orlando, Florida, and asked our son, President George W. Bush, if he thought it was important for families to sit down together at the dinner table and share meals. George replied, "I did eat with my family, so long as my mother wasn't cooking. Wait a minute... just kidding, Mom!... She was one of the great fast food cooks of all time. Just kidding, Mom! We ate a lot together. We did, and I think it's important to do that." Sitting right behind George was our Jeb, the Governor of Florida, trying very hard to keep a straight face.

Later, the two of them called me, wondering if I had been watching TV. Lucky for them, I had not seen it, and they were laughing so hard, they could hardly explain what had happened. They just thought it was too funny.

Caitlin sent me a letter apologizing for the whole thing. Well, I want you to know, Caitlin, it was a good question you asked and the President was only kidding.

Believe it or not, people still ask me about that little incident. OK, so the truth is out – I'm not the greatest cook in the world, but I did put dinner on the table for five children. But what's more important than what we ate, is the time we spent together. It was at the dinner table where we learned about each other's day, celebrated successes, and provided support for the disappointments. George and I are often asked if it was at the dinner table where we encouraged our children to run for public office, discussed world events, and pushed them all to achieve great things. Not exactly. It simply was the time of day when we came together as a family.

Unfortunately, I'm not sure family dinners are as prevalent as they were when our children were growing up. We've all gotten way too busy. The children are always dashing off for soccer games or to meet friends at the mall; parents get stuck late at the office or have to attend a meeting; and way too much attention is paid to television, cell phones, and all the other distractions that come with technology and convenience.

Do we ever just sit down and just talk to our children any more?

This concern is why I was thrilled to learn that the Kimball family was writing a book focused on the importance of eating meals together as a family. I hope you will enjoy their stories and think about the advice that they share. As you're reading this book, please keep in mind that for all of us who chose to have children, the most important job we will ever have is that of parent. Whether you are President of the United States, a teacher or a lawyer, a plumber or a CEO, our children must come first. Making the commitment to sit down to dinner as a family as many nights as possible is one way – and a fairly easy way – to make sure our children realize how much of a priority they are in our lives.

In my work with the Barbara Bush Foundation for Family Literacy, I've often said that I believe that the home is the child's first school and a parent is the child's first and most important teacher. You could say, then, that the dinner table is their first school desk. It is a place where children can talk to their parents and learn about who they are, and what their families believe in.

And while you're at it, please don't forget the importance of reading together either. Sharing a book with your child will help stir their imaginations and give them an early appreciation of reading and learning.

Eating together, reading together, spending time together – it's all about being a family together.  It will make your family stronger, and stronger families will make America stronger. It's that simple.

So please enjoy this wonderful book. I wish you and your family many happy meals together.

Sincerely,

*Barbara Bush*

Barbara Bush

# Chapter One
## Drawing Families Together, One Meal at a Time

### My Family Needs Help!

I can't believe it was only a few years ago that I found myself thinking that. My name is Jill Kimball, and my husband, Neal, and I were desperately trying to raise our four children in the midst of our hectic, daily lives. Neal was working just as hard as he could to make sure we had everything we needed, and I was working just as hard as I could to run the house and the kids in an efficient and loving manner, but it just kept on getting harder and harder… and no matter how hard we were working at keeping it all together, it felt like we were all slowly but surely drifting apart.

Does any of this sound familiar? Dad and/or Mom works hard every day, and some nights and weekends, your kids go off to school and all their after-school activities, and their soccer games on the weekends – and you're all trying to manage a household, trying to get your work done, and trying to keep the whole thing together. Meanwhile, the pressure of all the things that you *need* to do seem like they're combining and piling up and keeping you from doing the things you *want* to do. And I'm talking about the most basic wants, what you wanted to do when you decided to have kids, and that was that you wanted to be a *family*.

And when you finally get a chance to juggle everybody's schedule to the point were you can actually come home together at the same time, it sometimes feels more like a group of strangers gathering – not exactly what you always thought that your family would be like. That's how it was getting to be at our house, the Kimball house… until we decided that it was time to dial back, and take a little time to look at ourselves and decide who and what we wanted to be.

# The Problem

As I said… a few years ago we felt ourselves and our four children drifting away from each other, and becoming more disconnected with each passing day. The pressures of being on the road for his big-time corporate job kept Neal just a little distant from the rest of the family, and I was beginning to feel like I was essentially a single parent.

My kids were drifting away too, as they were getting older and getting more and more caught up in extra-curricular activities at school, and music lessons and sports teams… we just felt like they were becoming more disconnected from each other with every passing day.

But what could we do about it? Neal had to work long hours to keep the family well fed, clothed and housed. I had to step in and run the house and the kids almost by myself – it wasn't that Neal didn't want to help, but he needed to travel for his job. And as for the kids activities, we just wanted to give our children the opportunities that any parent wants to give their children – the chance to pursue their interests, to sate their natural curiosity, and the chance to participate in team sports.

The main problem was that we were spending so much time and energy on being the perfect providers for our family that we almost forgot how to BE a family.

I know this all sounds familiar to you, because I know you have kids and you're facing the same challenges that we were, and we continue to face everyday. If you didn't have a family in need of help, you wouldn't be reading this book!

Like most parents, you know you want the best of everything for your kids, and you're willing to work long hours to make sure they get it. But maybe they don't need the best of what money can buy. Maybe what they need the best of is *you*. Maybe they need just a little bit more of your time, a little more time for you to simply be a family.

# The Solution

**IDEA**

After we found ourselves in this vicious cycle of feeling time-crunched, or the need to keep up with the proverbial Joneses, we took a long hard look at what we were doing.

Things came to a head for us on a long family car trip. We realized we needed to do *something* that would enable us to reconnect as a family. And that *something* we needed to do was simple enough… we just needed to spend more time together and we needed to communicate.

Now I'm certain that like so many people, you're probably saying, "That sounds simple… but we just don't have the TIME." But unlike so many others, what I propose is not about MAKING time. That's impossible. What we decided was that we needed to stop trying to make time… but RECLAIM it.

Once we began thinking about it, we realized that the one big thing that was absent from our lives now that had been a cornerstone of the family when we were kids was the simple family dinner. That sort of "and how was your day" conversation around a pot roast that had kept everything together back in our own childhood.

But that sort of family meal just wasn't possible with our schedules. So we decided to commit to eating *AT LEAST* one family meal together a week. But not just ANY meal… we were going to make that meal a special one.

**TOGETHER**

> **What is important here is not the quantity of meals… though obviously the more, the better. But what we wanted was at least one QUALITY meal where we could come together and truly bond as a family should.**

Together in 1999, with our kids Caitlin, 11; Maggie, 9; Kyle, 6; and five-year-old Jimmy, we got together as a family and created what we now know as *Family Table Time* – an interactive tool to make mealtimes more fun, while all the time bringing more focus to the occasion and ultimately helping to bring the family closer together. The centerpiece of the kit is a large vinyl tablecloth that provides a foundation for the family meetings. The tablecloth becomes a living journal, where family members jot down ideas, record experiences, catalog values, feelings and set goals. Included in the package are "Weekly Meeting Recipes," permanent colored markers, the "Get Cookin' *Family Table Time* Prep" for using the kit effectively, Quick Start Plates, and a certificate of commitment for each family member to sign. A "Mealtime Measuring Cup" records the number of days the family eats dinner together and there's a spot for you to list values and beliefs that are important to your family.

And the kit worked like a charm. Everybody slowed down for the mealtime, and for the family meeting that followed those special meals. It was like we were getting off the freeway of life and taking the scenic route! We felt like we were more connected as a family and we finally felt like we really knew our kids. And the kids feel like they really knew their parents too. And we've made the Kimball household into a real family – just like the one we had always hoped to be.

# What is *Family Table Time?*

It was during that fateful family road trip in 1999 that we came up with the idea for *Family Table Time*. We were looking for a way to better communicate with each other and the family mealtime seemed to be the logical place to start. But the question was how to make our time together meaningful and fun. Through trial and error, we developed an interactive, yet simple tool: *Family Table Time*. And in the process, we found that we had created a way for families to plan family activities, build core values, strengthen family unity, and create positive family memories.

**MEAL TIME**

Now, in this book *Drawing Families Together, One Meal at a Time*, we're partnering with our friends Drs. Stacey and Michael Dunn to bring the lessons we've learned around our dinner table to other families. With this book, we will try to lay out a framework to help other modern families become reconnected. Drawing on the experiences of *Family Table Time* kit users, and supported by the clinical knowledge of friends, fellow parents and psychologists, Stacey and Michael Dunn, we're putting together a book that we feel will become an essential parenting tool for other busy parents. This is designed to help other harried parents reconnect with their own families… one meal at a time.

# Meet the Kimballs:

We're just like many other families you know, and we've shared a lot of the same experiences you have. My youth was spent in one town in New Jersey with wonderful parents and an older brother and younger sister. I graduated in 1982 with a BA from Providence College in Rhode Island. Before giving up my career to become a full-time stay-at-home Mom to my four children, I sold television airtime in the advertising industry. (I used to say **B.C.** I sold **air** - **B**efore **C**hildren!)

My husband, Neal Kimball, graduated from the University of South Florida in 1979. He worked for 24 years with Fortune 100 Companies, relocating 9 times during those years, before leaving to start our own company, Family Communications Institute, Inc. Neal has helped me by bringing the wealth of his experience, not to mention his strong values from his family.

Neal grew up in Tampa, Florida, and came from a close-knit family as well. He had great parents and five brothers and sisters. We met in 1985 and married in 1986. Four children came along, and job responsibilities increased – and Neal experienced first-hand the demands and pressure that corporate life can have on a family. There never seemed to be enough time to just talk with each other. We both remember and value the discussions around the dinner table and how they were a focal point of our family life.

When the demands of corporate life caused us to question what was really important, we resolved to take our family back – and we decided that mealtime was going to be the place. To make our time together more meaningful and fun, we developed *Family Table Time*. What began as our idea to help our family re-knit has become what we believe is a way for all families to plan activities, build values and strengthen family unity.

# Meet the Dunns:

Dr. Michael E. Dunn and Dr. Stacey Tantleff-Dunn are first and foremost, good family friends.

Michael is currently an Associate Professor of Psychology and Director of the Substance Use Research Group at the University of Central Florida, and a Licensed Psychologist in the State of Florida. He is also the founder and President of University Prevention Consultants, Inc., a company that provides expert consulting to colleges, universities, and other institutions on substance abuse prevention and treatment. His training includes an M.A. and Ph.D. in Clinical Psychology and a Post-Doctoral Fellowship in alcohol and substance use research. He has published and presented over 100 scientific papers on alcohol and substance use, he has completed numerous program evaluations of substance abuse treatment and prevention programs, he has served as a grant reviewer for the National Institute on Alcohol Abuse and Alcoholism, and he serves as a reviewer for numerous scientific journals. He even teaches graduate courses in the clinical doctoral program at UCF in substance abuse treatment, research methods, statistics, and psychotherapy. He has served as a substance abuse prevention and treatment consultant to school districts, colleges, attorneys, and community organizations. Dr. Dunn's research interests include cognitive development related to substance use and outcome expectancies, prevention of substance abuse among children and young adults, and treatment of substance use disorders.

Dr. Stacey Tantleff-Dunn completed a B.A. in Psychology at the George Washington University before earning her M.A. and Ph.D. in Clinical Psychology at the University of South Florida. She has worked in a university counseling center, a VA medical center, and has been a member of the faculty at two universities. Dr. Dunn is a Licensed Clinical Psychologist and is currently an associate professor at the University of Central Florida and is the director of the Laboratory for the Study of Eating, Appearance, and Health (LEAH) at UCF. She teaches graduate and undergraduate courses in individual and group psychotherapy, eating disorders, abnormal psychology, and interpersonal communication and relationship enhancement. She has published a book, numerous journal articles and contributed to other books as well. She has also served as a body image and eating disorders consultant to several organizations. Dr. Dunn also has a private practice specializing in body image, adolescent issues, relationship enhancement, and couples and family therapy.

At the time of this writing, the Drs. Dunn have a four-year-old daughter, Nicole, and another child on the way.

Needless to say, these two wonderfully talented people have provided a wealth of information over the years that have given us the ability to strengthen what we've learned. Their experience and guidance has allowed us to be better parents. And it is their example that inspired us to take what we learned and try to show others how to reclaim their families as well.

# Trial and Error

The trial and error part of the development process began when we spoke to our pastor in Chicago, which is where we were going on that fateful family road trip. We told the pastor what we were thinking about doing, and he thought it was a wonderful idea.
Much to our surprise, we quickly found out that most of our old friends in the Chicago suburbs were in the same boat! With the help of our pastor, we organized some meetings in the recreation room of our former church, and invited some of those families to come in and speak with us. The main feedback we received in those initial meetings was that most families:

✔ Wanted to get their spouse home for dinner

✔ Wanted to get their teenager/s to talk

✔ Felt like they were strong, but in need of some guidance

✔ Had heard of family meetings but no one really told them how to do them

**FUN FACT**

So we shared our ideas with our friends and asked them to test out the idea of *Family Table Time* – which was basically coming back to the dinner table, meeting together at the dinner table once a week to have a meal together, and the *Family Table Time* meeting. The families were given twelve weeks of agendas for their *Family Table Time* meeting, a vinyl tablecloth and indelible markers and asked to create and write their own Family Vision statement in the center and to meet once a week over a meal, have a meeting and for every family member to write, draw a memory of the week on their tablecloth. All nineteen families that attended the initial meeting agreed to test out the concept!

The stories we heard when we came back and saw the tablecloths told us that we were definitely on the right track. Parents were seeing how beneficial the once a week meeting was and started coming home more often for dinner together during the week. Teenagers reportedly loved running the meeting, and enjoyed finding out just what everyone else in their family was up to and everyone loved writing on the tablecloth!

# Support From the First Family

As we continued to develop our *Family Table Time* idea, we found out that a member of a pretty famous family was thinking right along the same lines. At a "town meeting" in Orlando, FL, shortly after the September 11th terrorist attacks, our daughters Caitlin and Maggie asked a question to President George W. Bush. Here's how the exchange went:

**EXAMPLE**

**President Bush**: Yes, ma'am?
**Caitlin**: Hi, Mr. President.

**President Bush**: I'm not nervous if you are.
**Caitlin**: Oh! I wrote it out because I thought I would be nervous. And I'm here with my sister Maggie and my family.

**President Bush**: Good... Hi, Maggie.
**Caitlin**: And I'm Caitlin. Our family wants to help out our country, and we think that making families strong will make our country strong. My parents believe that eating meals together will do that. Is this something that you did when you were a kid and that you and Mrs. Bush believe in?

**President Bush**: "I did eat with my family so long as my mother wasn't cooking. Wait a minute... just kidding, Mom! She was one of the great fast food cooks of all time. Just kidding, Mom! We ate a lot together. We did, and I think it's important to do that. I think that's a very interesting question."

"You know, we live in a society that's a busy society. We live in a society where it's so easy to forget the fundamentals. But one of the really positive things that have come out of the evil of 9/11 was that people are beginning to ask, you know, "What's important? What's important?"

"I think you've touched on something really important, and that's family. And the idea of a mom and dad prioritizing family is all about not only enhancing the quality of life of their children but collectively making America so much stronger and so much better after the evils. This is an unbelievably great country we live in. The values of America are so strong, and the people are so real and so good. And 9/11 has brought out, in many instances, the best in America, and part of that are the decisions individual families make about setting new priorities in their lives."

After that exchange, we decided it was really time to pursue this *Family Table Time* idea, and embarked on getting the word out to as many people as possible. We started doing radio interviews, newspaper articles and interviews, extended speaking engagements and now we're working on this book with our friends the Dunns.

## The Kimballs and Dunns Working Together

While we knew from anecdotal experiences that families eating together would help strengthen family ties and raise better-adjusted kids, the Dunns are trained specialists and doctors in the field of psychology and they are experts in the science and statistics *behind* the ideas. And we've found that specific studies have been done over the years highlighting the benefits of time spent together at the dinner table. Here are a few examples:

**TOGETHER**

✔ Research by CASA (The National Center on Addiction and Substance Abuse) and other organizations has shown that teens that eat frequent family dinners are less likely than other teens to smoke, drink, use illegal drugs, have sex at young ages, get into fights or be suspended from school. And these results hold true regardless of a teen's sex, family structure or socioeconomic level.

✔ In a research project conducted by Dr. Blake Bowden of Cincinnati Children's Hospital Center, 527 teenagers were studied to determine what family and lifestyle characteristics were related to good mental health and adjustment. Dr. Bowden and his colleagues found that kids who ate dinner with their families at least five times per week (at home or in a fast food restaurant) were the least likely to take drugs, feel depressed or get into trouble with the law. In addition, these young people were more likely to do well in school and to have a supportive circle of friends. The more poorly adjusted teens, in contrast, ate with their parents an average of three or fewer evenings a week

✔ A survey conducted by the University of Chicago revealed that a majority of graduate students, when asked where they got most of their ideas about morality and religion, responded "through conversation with the family at meal times."

✔ One Harvard University study links children's literacy and school success to explanatory talk at the dinner table – for instance, discussions of presidential politics or the day's news. Not only does that expand a child's world but it also helps a child learn to handle differences of opinion, negotiate ways to get into a conversation, hear new vocabulary words, and predict and anticipate parents' reactions.

✔ A 1996 study done by Dr. Catherine Snow, a professor of education at Harvard's Graduate School of Education, revealed similar results. By following 65 families over an eight-year period, it was determined that dinnertime was of more value to child development than playtime, school and story time. Clearly, there is power in family fellowship.

✔ A study several years ago found that the most common trait of high school National Merit Scholars was that they grew up eating dinner together as a family.

✔ In *Talking With Teens: The YMCA Parent and Teen Survey Final Report*, 78 percent of youth indicated that they turn to their parents for advice and guidance in times of need.

✔ The YMCA survey also found that not having enough time with their parents is the top concern of young people. Youth were three times as likely as their parents to indicate that family time is their biggest issue of concern. Parents reported outside threats such as drugs and alcohol as their top concerns.

✔ The article, Protecting Adolescents From Harm: Findings From the National Longitudinal Study on Adolescent Health, in the *Journal of the American Medical Association*, reported that parent and family connectedness help to protect adolescents from seven of the eight harmful behaviors examined.

✔ In *Teens and Their Parents in the 21st Century: An Examination of Trends in Teen Behavior and the Role of Parental Involvement*, the Council of Economic Advisors indicated that parental involvement is a major influence in helping youth avoid risky behaviors, such as drug use and early sexual activity. In addition, young people who have a close relationship with their parents are more likely to have higher grade point averages and to go to college.

✔ And finally, research conducted by the Drs. Dunn on students entering their freshman year of college found that eating meals together as a family corresponded to lower rates of depression, lower levels of alcohol use, lower levels of marijuana use, lower levels of cigarette use, lower levels of illicit drug use, higher self-esteem, better grades, and lower levels of suspension and detention.

Now, eating dinner with your children is certainly not a guarantee that your kids will be National Merit Scholars, and sail through life with no problems, but it does seem like the experts are all in agreement that it's a good start.

# We Are a Family

*Communication, Collaboration, Cooperation and Family Self-Esteem*

There are several immediate benefits that can result from sitting down to dinner with your children. The first, and most obvious, is increased communication. When kids are younger they will tell you every little detail of their lives. Anyone who has ever parented a teenager knows how difficult it can be to get them to give more than one-word answers to questions. One way we learned to increase communication was letting those sullen teenagers express their thoughts by writing on the tablecloth. And why not? Any communication is better than long moody silences, and any sort of communication can open the door to a deeper sharing of feelings, thoughts and concerns.

Some important points to remember are that communication is a two-way street. Don't expect your kids to communicate with you unless they feel that you are a full-time collaborator in this venture. If they're opening up and talking, you need to cooperate and collaborate in the process in a 100% fashion.

Nothing fosters a sense of belonging, love and self-esteem like family communication. It can generate confidence, promote exploration… and result in discovery. It can even engage children with developmental disorders such as autism. As the level of communication rises, you'll notice a rise in the level of your general family self-esteem… you'll start to feel like more of a family – however you choose to define that word – than ever before.

Remember, this is just an introductory chapter, to help you get a feel of who the authors are, where we're coming from, and just what sort of things you can hope to accomplish from applying the principles and guidelines in this book. We'll examine the concepts of *Communication, Collaboration, Cooperation and Family Self-Esteem* more fully in the upcoming chapters. We'll also address specific issues facing today's families, and give you a good handle on how to discuss sensitive topics.

# A Little Pep Talk

You've made a good start, just by picking up this book. *Drawing Families Together, One Meal at a Time* is about helping families share and communicate with each other on a regular basis at the dinner table. Our goal is not only to bring families to the table for meals – where both parents and kids have the opportunity to share what's important in their lives – but also to help you bring structure and order to your family life.

The time you have with your children is fleeting. You want them to be happy and loving, and give them the tools they will need for their future. Many books promote family meals as a tool for developing communication and social skills. Why is this one unique? This book is a practical tool to help you do precisely that. Listening is important, and having a strong family is more than just living in the same house together and catching an occasional meal together; it takes effort.

Partnering together with the Dunns, we have made it our mission to share with other families the importance of the time spent together as a family and how it will affect their children and society as a whole.

These days, everyone in the family is busy, and there never seems to be enough time to connect. Many families in the 21st Century serve their meals buffet style – with separate seatings for Dad, Mom and the kids, and eat in front of the TV. But it wasn't always this way.

The family table used to be a central place in any home – and dinnertime was sacred. No one missed dinner – no one wanted to – because this was the time set aside for family discussion. Problems were brought up, and resolved. Family issues were addressed, plans for future activities were made, and some wise aleck made cracks about Mom's cooking… just like President Bush!

If you wanted to go to the dance on Saturday, the family dinner table was where you made your request. If you planned on taking the family on vacation to Disney World, this is where plans were discussed. Remember the Waltons? Who didn't want to join their family at the table?

Well, not everyone can be the Waltons and we're not even suggesting that everybody would want to be like the Waltons. But we're fairly certain that everybody would like to open the lines of family communication wide, and to start functioning as the sort of family you've always dreamed of being. The lessons contained in this book are designed to help you do just that.

# Jumpstart Your *Family Table Time*

While you're reading this book, you can get started on the fast track to family communication. While it is not necessary to buy the kit in order to learn the valuable problem-solving and communication skills we will cover in this book, it is a valuable took that can help bring your family together.

**IDEA**

So if you feel that your family is becoming fractured, and you don't want to lose any more valuable time before you begin to reconnect, you may want to reinstate the wisdom of bringing your family together right away. *Family Table Time* will help you do just that. To order a *Family Table Time* kit, please visit www.familytabletime.com.

Now, let's get started!

# Chapter One

# Chapter Two
## What Will Bring Your Family Together?

## Bringing Your Family Together

We use what we call *"Family Table Time"* as a system to bring our family together over the dinner table – using this time to communicate with each other, offer praise, resolve issues, and make future family plans.

If you can commit to sharing at least one sit-down meal with your kids a week, as a family, you'll be able to share in some of the benefits we've seen in our kids. And we've found that if you start communicating with your children more closely at an early age, they will be more willing to share in their typically unresponsive teenage years.

Meals are an important tool to help in the learning of social skills. Our kids developed important social skills during family meals, such as minding their manners, taking their turns to speak and actually listening when another person is talking.

Most of the authorities in the field agree that families can improve the quality of their lives by allowing children aged two and older to participate in some family discussions. This gives children a sense of importance and encourages them to cooperate. Predictable experiences give children a feeling of control. The best mechanism of this is a family meeting. What better place to begin that communication than at your family table?

**TOGETHER**

**QUOTES**

> ## Eating together is important because:
>
> ✔ Experts agree that family dinner table conversation has been shown to increase children's mental and verbal abilities.
> ✔ Eating together promotes good communication, and strengthens family bonds and relationships.
> ✔ Families who regularly eat together have more cohesion and unity.
> ✔ Family meals give children a sense of security.

Since 1996, research by The National Center on Addiction and Substance Abuse at Columbia University has consistently shown that the more often a child eats dinner with his family, the less likely that child is to smoke, drink or use illegal drugs. This research is published in CASA's annual Teen Surveys, which are available in the publications section of its Web site, www.casacolumbia.org. The key findings on family dinners appear in the surveys from 1998, 1999 and 2000.

The National Center on Addiction and
Substance Abuse at Columbia University

# What Family Meals Can Help You Achieve

There are literally hundreds of books on parenting lining the shelves of your local bookstore. You've all seen the books that offer advice and tips on setting limits, how to teach responsibility, how to instill discipline, how to teach family values, building character, and just generally protecting kids from risky and unhealthy sorts of behaviors.

Of course these are all vital and critical concerns to parents who are taking their parenting role seriously. But who has time to read all those books?

The whole point of this book is that parents can get so overwhelmed by the pressures of everyday life that they forget to take the time to do the things they need to do to create a family. Remember, anybody can have kids but it takes parents to make a family. And most of what you need to do you already know. It's not locked away in a book somewhere – it's right inside of you!

You see, Neal and I have found out that not all good parenting tips are complex, or hard to understand. Not all good parenting tips require dramatic changes in priorities or lifestyle. The love you feel for your children is all you really need to begin to build a stronger family.

Children who feel loved thrive physically, emotionally, socially and intellectually. It is important for children to feel connected to their parents, to have a sense of belonging. Some believe that kids who have that connection with their parents have an easier time forming relationships, do better in school, respect authority, and tend not to experiment with drugs, alcohol, and sex. It is so important to build a solid relationship as a family!

> "Research has shown that teens who eat frequent family dinners are less likely than other teens to get into fights or be suspended from school. They are also at lower risk for thoughts of suicide. Frequent family dining is also correlated with doing well in school and developing healthy eating habits."
>
> Michael Duffy, assistant secretary for Louisiana's Department of Health and Hospital's Office for Addictive Disorders.

QUOTES

Many other books promote family meals as a tool for developing communication and social skills, but this book is a practical guide that will actually *help* you do this. It gives you an opportunity to *listen* to your children.

According to many recent surveys, less than half the families in the United States actually sit down to a meal together on a regular basis. Yet, all the reading I have done and just about every expert I have heard speak end up all saying just about the same thing: family meals are strongly related to the development of your children's mental health and stability. Everybody thinks it's a good idea: a Harvard Medical School study found there are nutritional, as well as social, emotional and academic advantages that occur in children when families share meals together.

**FUN FACT**

"Children who eat dinner with their parents tend to eat healthier meals that are lower in saturated fat, and higher in fiber, fruit and vegetables than when unsupervised."

Karen Miller-Kovach, Chief Scientist
at Weight Watchers International.

# The Benefits of Family Meals

Children who eat regular meals with their parents show some shared characteristics. I'm sure you'll all agree that you'd be happy to get the results listed below:

✔ They show appreciation for family members by giving each other compliments and try to make everyone feel appreciated and good about themselves.

✔ They have the ability to deal with crises in a positive manner.

✔ They spend time together. In all areas of their lives, they structure their schedules so that they can spend time together.

✔ They have a high degree of commitment to families. They invest time and energy in each other to make family their number one priority.

✔ They have good communication patterns. These families spend time talking with each other and they listen well, which shows respect.

✔ They have a high degree of spiritual orientation. A spiritual lifestyle tends to make them more forgiving, patient and positive.

**MEAL TIME**

Accomplish this by encouraging family members to:

✔ Commit to ongoing family meals and meetings.

✔ Share ownership of these meetings (each family member has a turn).

✔ Document happenings, progress, family guests, and even a family "Vision Statement" on your tablecloth or somewhere prominent in your family's mealtimes.

✔ Communicate in a structured (but fun) manner.

The result of ongoing family meetings like this is greater family harmony.

Aside from the obvious benefits of talking with our kids more, such as really finding out what's going on in their lives on a day-to-day basis, we've also found out that time spent around our dinner table has had far-reaching benefits we hadn't expected.

Just the simple act of committing to the time it takes to make a family meal, you can end up creating something healthier than what you would normally eat. A survey of middle and high school students, as reported in the March 2003 Journal of the American Dietetic Association, determined that teens that ate family meals more frequently also had healthier diets. The results found that kids who ate family meals actually drank less soda and ate more fruits, vegetables, grains and calcium-rich foods!

QUOTES

A University of Minnesota study in a recent issue of the *Journal of the American Dietetic Association* showed that researchers found that children aged 11 to 18 who joined their families for meals ate more fruits, vegetables, grains, and nutrient-dense foods than adolescents who ate separately from their families. The study also found that teens who sat down to at least seven family meals a week ate fewer snack foods than teens who took part in fewer family meals. Boys ate more family meals than girls, and middle school kids ate more family meals than high school students.

Methodist Health Care System of Houston, TX

So eating together not only is good for the mental and emotional health of your family, it's also good for their physical well-being as well.

# Your Family Meal and Meeting

### What is it?

With all this talk about sitting down as a family and eating meals, you're probably wondering just what else a family meal and meeting brings to the table. Well, it's a little more than simply slapping a pizza down on the table and talking about your respective days.

What Neal and I have found is that we can combine a family meal with a family meeting and really make the most of the time we sit down at the dinner table. So this is what *Family Table Time* really is: a consistent time each week, decided on as a family, where the family meets at the table to share a meal, and then to discuss important issues, feelings, activities, and to connect with each other.

As we noted previously, experts have said that families can improve the quality of their lives by allowing children aged two and older to participate in some family discussions. This gives children a sense that they are important in the family and it encourages them to open up and cooperate. Also, "predictable experiences" give children a feeling of control – in the case of family meetings, predicable experiences can be a sort of ritual, and I'll discuss the importance of family rituals later in this chapter.

Please remember that it is important to be realistic of what to expect with the age of your children. Maybe a 10-minute meeting is what will work for younger children. As we all know, it's almost impossible to get younger kids to sit down for longer! Don't give up! Stay at the table, make it fun-fun-fun and the kids will come back asking for more.

**TOGETHER**

> ## How to get the most out of the Time Together
>
> ✔ **Meet at the table for a meal.**
>
> ✔ **Talk and share your experiences and feelings.**
>
> ✔ **Listen, be open... this is discovery time!**

# Tips for Making Family Meals a Pleasant Experience

Make mealtimes a fun experience, something that your kids will look forward to. Try to share funny stories that happened to you and talk about things that may actually be of interest to your kids.

**IDEA**

✔ One thing to avoid is using time spent at the family table as an opportunity to criticize your kids by putting them on the spot about an uncompleted chore or unfinished homework.

✔ Think about just how long your kids can realistically sit still for; don't try to make the meal time and the meeting last too long... especially for the first few times.

✔ This is a biggie: turn off the television and the computer.

✔ No telephone calls during dinner – let the answering machine/voicemail get it. If you don't have an answering machine, don't worry. They'll call back, and it was probably just a telemarketer anyway. The same rule applies for both kids and parents!

✔ Mom and Dad should avoid talking to each other about adult-only issues. Leave that for after the kids go to bed.

✔ Even if your kids are too young to really participate, begin family meals now, just so they get used to the whole idea and they get used to parent/child communication at the table.

✔ If you haven't been eating family dinners weekly, try and ease into the new routine. Older kids like teens and adolescents may really resist if they see it as forced family time that cuts into their personal schedules. It wouldn't hurt to invite their friends to join you around the dinner table from time to time.

✔ Don't give up too easily! Believe me, we know that between work, school, sports and whatever other activities that the kids and the parents are involved in it can be a real hassle to cast a family dinnertime in stone at least once a week. Keep trying and working toward the goal. One meal together is better than none!

✔ Maybe your family mealtime and meeting can be a breakfast, lunch or brunch. It could be at a restaurant too!

**MEAL TIME**

# Developing Long Term Family Goals

### What is a Family Vision Statement?

One of the most important things you will do during your family meals and meetings is to create long-term goals for your family communication efforts. In the *Family Table Time* Kit, Neal and I call this a Family Vision Recipe. For this book, we'll use the term "Family Vision Statement." Simply put, this is something that articulates your family's purpose and direction. A Family Vision Statement creates a unified environment, a reference point for all family members. A good Vision Statement inspires and imparts a sense of stability.

## Tips for Creating a Family Vision Statement:

Make sure that everyone in the family helps decide on a Family Vision Statement. You'll never achieve your mission if it's not something everybody wants to work towards.

**REMEMBER**

> *Write your Family Vision Statement down and display it somewhere prominent near your dinner table. That way you can always reference it during your family meals and meetings.*
> **(HINT: We use a special tablecloth with our family)**

Here are some helpful things to remember when you're working on your Family Vision Statement.

✔ It should be a statement that helps to explain why your family exists and should include a vision of the sort of family you want to become.

✔ It should provide an opportunity for growth for your family

✔ Be realistic! Don't make your statement too grand, or you'll never feel like your making any progress.

✔ Try and make your vision measurable, so your family can see the steps that you are making all the way until your goal.

✔ Make it inspirational for your family, so that all of you feel better about yourselves as you're working towards achieving your Family Vision Statement.

# Creating Your Family Vision Statement

> Creating a Vision Statement will be, without question, one of
> the most powerful and significant things you will ever do to
> take leadership of your life. In it you will identify the first, most
> important roles, relationships, and things in your life – who
> you want to be, what you want to do, to whom and what you
> want to give your life, the principles you want to anchor your
> life to, the legacy you want to leave. All the goals and decisions
> you will make in the future will be based upon it. It's like
> deciding first which wall you want to lean your ladder of life
> against, and then beginning to climb. It will be a compass – a
> strong source of guidance amid the stormy seas and pressing,
> pulling currents of your life.
> -Dr. Stephen R. Covey

QUOTES

In his book, *The 7 Habits of Highly Effective Families*, Dr. Stephen Covey
has dedicated an entire chapter on how to create a family Vision
Statement. He believes a family Vision Statement gives a family a
*destination* and a *compass*. Neal and I found this chapter to be very
helpful to us when we were just starting out.

Creating a Family Vision Statement will probably be a major topic at a
few of your early family meetings. You are creating a statement that
says who your family is, what you will live by and what you will stand
for. This is something the whole family should be involved in to get the
maximum commitment from all involved. If there is no involvement,
there will be little or no commitment.

**EXAMPLE**

To help get your family started, try beginning your Family Vision Statement with some of these starter words:

✔ Our family dream is....

✔ My greatest wish for my family is....

✔ The purpose of my family is....

✔ The way I describe my family is....

✔ Our family focus should be....

✔ I am grateful for....

✔ I am happy when....

✔ Our family provides to others by....

✔ Our family likes to....

✔ Other families we admire are....

✔ We admire them because....

✔ My responsibilities as a family member are...

✔ Our family heroes are...

✔ We like them because....

✔ I like our home because....

✔ Relationships with others are important to me because....

✔ Some unique talents and gifts my family has are....

✔ Others describe our family as....

✔ I would like our family to be remembered as....

✔ Values that are important to our family are....

At your first family meeting, have the family discuss these ideas as well as your own. Take your time, be open, listen and make sure you write down all ideas. Now you are ready to create your Family Vision Statement.

Your Vision Statement can be in sentence form or a picture, as long as it represents the family as a whole and everyone is on board. Write your mission statement in the present tense. For example, instead of *To live a life full of love, work and play and kindness to others...*, write *Living a life...* instead. This way you are making your vision a reality instead of a future goal.

# The Importance of Creating Family Rituals

There's been a ton of research done over the last fifty years on how important family routines and rituals are to the healthy development of children. There's even one article that sums up all the research nicely, and Neal and I used this piece when we were trying to understand the difference between rituals and routine and figure out just how important rituals and routine were to our family's development. You can find that article online, if you'd like to read it in its entirety at: www.apa.org/journals/fan/press_releases/december_2002/fam164381.pdf

The article is called *A Review of 50 Years of Research on Naturally Occurring Family Routines and Rituals: Cause for Celebration?*, Barbara H. Fiese, Thomas J. Tomcho, Michael Douglas, Kimberly Josephs, Scott Poltrock, and Tim Baker; Syracuse University; *Journal of Family Psychology*, Vol. 16, No. 4.

Of the 32 studies reviewed in this article, one of the more common routines identified was dinnertime. The most frequently identified family rituals were birthdays, Christmas, family reunions, Easter, Passover, Thanksgiving, funerals and Sunday activities including the "Sunday dinner."

The Sunday dinner... doesn't that sound like one special dinner a week, or just what Neal and I do with our kids during our family meals and meetings? We've taken one dinner a week and raised it from the level of routine and placed it in the realm of ritual.

Psychologist Barbara H. Fiese, Ph.D., and her colleagues at Syracuse University began their article by explaining the difference between a family routine and a family ritual.

**QUOTES**

"Routines involve instrumental communication conveying information that 'this is what needs to be done' and involve a momentary time commitment so that once the act is completed, there is little, if any, afterthought. Rituals, on the other hand, involve symbolic communication and convey 'this is who we are' as a group and provide continuity in meaning across generations. Also, there is often an emotional imprint where once the act is completed, the individual may replay it in memory to recapture some of the positive experience."

Barbara H. Fiese, Ph.D

So just what does that mean in English, and what does it mean to us? Well, one of the objects of this whole book is to help you create a Family Vision Statement – a statement that says "this is who we are." So, in effect, when you take that one family meal a week and apply the principles you learn by reading this book you're creating a family ritual, one that is unique to your family. It makes it pretty special when you look at it in that light, doesn't it?

# How to Create a Family Ritual

Any routine has the potential to become a ritual once it moves from an instrumental to a symbolic act. An instrumental act would be setting the table for dinner – but it becomes a symbolic act when you're setting the table for a *special* meal. When you're getting ready for your special family meal, do things just a little bit differently. Make it obvious – just like when your kids see a menorah and know it's Chanukah, or when they see a Christmas tree and know it's Christmas, when they see your table set in a certain way they'll know it's time for a special family dinner and meeting. Just like that, you've elevated the simple routine of putting plates on a table into a family ritual.

**REMEMBER**

## Some other tips on how to create Family Rituals:

✔ Begin to excite interest in the meal before anyone even sits down at the table. Involve the entire family by assigning each member a task, whether it's setting the table, making a salad, carrying stuff to the table or even just helping put the ingredients near the stove. That way everyone will feel like they played a role in the meal preparation process.

✔ Candles are always cool, and kids love them. Small gestures like candles can signal the importance of gathering together around the table. Try lighting several candles on the dinner table when your special meal begins and blowing them out when it ends to signify the beginning and end of the meal and family meeting.

✔ Turn even the smallest and seemingly insignificant events into special occasions by celebrating milestones or achievements like losing a tooth, getting a hit or scoring a goal, or even just not striking out, or getting a good grade on a pop quiz.

✔ By constantly using the dinner table as a place to celebrate, parents and kids alike will look forward to having dinner together more often.

✔ Encourage family members to take turns suggesting a topic of discussion at each meal so everyone feels involved and valued.

✔ Some weeks a family member picks a theme for our special meal. We once had a "back to school" meal and meeting. Our daughter, Caitlin served our dinner in brown paper bags and made place cards with chalk and black construction paper. We have had backwards nights, where we have had dessert first; movie nights; pajama nights; etc.

# Don't Worry, You're Doing Great!

Don't start to feel overwhelmed by all this talk about family meetings and routines and rituals. I just want to remind you that Neal and I were once in the same position as you find yourself in right now. We were good parents, working as hard as we possibly could to make a better life for our kids, and we just felt ourselves drifting further and further apart under all the pressures that are put on a modern family.

**THERE IS NO SUCH THING AS A PERFECT FAMILY.**

So don't beat yourself up over any problems you may have. The "perfect family" is a myth, and not what we're striving for here. For us, things started to get better once we committed to having that one special family dinner a week. And that's all we can ever really achieve... a BETTER family... not a "perfect" one.

Because of our family meals our kids know us as well as we knew our parents when we were growing up! This return to old-fashioned values in our modern world is not only preferred, we feel it is necessary. The kids are all doing fine, and Neal and I are feeling a lot better about where we are headed as a family… and you can feel the same about your family too.

So, don't get overwhelmed and decide to quit before you even start. You're on the right track. Keep reading and start acting on the things that you learn. Slowly but surely you'll begin to see the same sort of results Neal and I have seen in our family.

# Chapter Three
## All Families Are Different

## Our Families Aren't the Same

One thing needs to be stated for the record... my family and your family are *not* the same. In fact, some days I feel like my family's not the same family it was the day before. Regardless, the point is that all families have their own special structure, communication, dynamics, etc. They are *all* different.

That's fine! Every family is different – some differences are very obvious, and some are not so obvious. But every family will be different, and should be different. It would be a very boring world if that weren't the case. Your family and my family won't be alike.

The good news is that while our families may be ever changing... experiences, problems and, most importantly, the resolutions will be quite similar. So don't worry if some of the examples don't hit home 100%. The "meat" of what we have to offer will be there for your specific family mealtime. And you will be able to extract what works for your specific circumstances.

But getting back to the differences in families... that is an important topic, because not so long ago, many families *were* quite similar. So it's worth looking at how the family has changed over the years.

**QUOTES**

> The structure of the American family has been undergoing vast transformations over the past 50 years. The year 2000 marked the first time when under one-quarter of U.S. households (23.5%) were made up of nuclear families, a married man and woman and their children, down from 45 percent of households in 1960. In the 1960s, 61 percent of families consisted of a father working out of the house, a homemaker mother and three children. The changing patterns of household formation, labor force participation and divorce and fertility rates have contributed to the transformation of family structure.
>
> Stephanie Sado and Angela Bayer of
> the Population Resource Center

What we think of as the classic American family is changing all the time, and the idea that you need a Mommy and a Daddy and a few kids to make up a family is not as prevalent as it once was. And families with the Mommy staying at home with an apron on, just like in *Leave It to Beaver*, are becoming fewer and fewer. Although lots of families would prefer that one parent stayed home with the kids, it's just not an economic reality for many of us.

In 1970, 43.3% of American women were active members of the labor force, working either part or full-time. By 1999, 60% of women were working and studies project that an increase in participation will continue. This rise in women's labor force participation has played a role in altering the structure of the American family. The increased presence of both parents in the labor force has contributed to the increase in median household income. In 1998, 65% of all married couples consisted of both the mother and the father earning a salary, compared to 1985 when this was the case for only 57% of married-couple families.

Stephanie Sado and Angela Bayer of
the Population Resource Center

QUOTES

Besides the fact that more mothers are working today, more women are waiting until they get a little more settled until they have kids. In 1997, the majority of women were giving birth between the ages of 25 and 29. In 1980, women ages 20 to 24 had the highest birth rate. This might swing back the other way in a few years, but it's just another way of showing that the traditional American family is changing even as you read this book. And that's okay!

There are lots of different reasons for this shift in American families lately. For a lot of younger families, it's just not economically practical to think in terms of a "family wage" – meaning there would not be enough income from *one* wage earner to support a family, the children's education and the couple's retirement. More and more younger families (and many older ones) now assume that the wife and mother can – and must – be an economic contributor to the family. It's just a fact that family income has dropped over the last decade and a half, unless there is a second earner.

**FUN FACT**

In February, 1988, the Congressional Budget Office released a report: "Trends in Family Income: 1970-1986." Staff of the U.S. House of Representatives' Select Committee on Children, Youth and Families analyzed these findings and concluded that although "family income for the typical family rose during this period… income gains were not evenly distributed. Low income families with children, young families at all income levels and poor single mother families in 1986 were much worse off than their counterparts in 1970." The main reason family incomes rose was "the increased number of workers per family, not increased earnings by the typical worker. Many families with children have needed to have both parents work to avoid losing ground."

> Arvonne S. Fraser, Senior Fellow at the Humphrey
> Institute of Public Affairs, University of Minnesota.

Even if the family wage concept was still applicable to most families, the increase in the divorce rate (and the record of support and maintenance awards and payments after divorce) may have led women of all ages to believe that there are no public or private guarantees of economic support in exchange for carrying out the traditional Mom role. Simply put, having a job outside the home may be well on its way to becoming the accepted form of self-insurance for women as well as men. And fringe benefits such as health insurance and social security have become an almost mandatory element of feeling self-sufficient.

But the whole thing still seems a little unfair to women. While today's women have moved into the paid workforce in such numbers that employment is no longer gender-based, women still seem to be primarily responsible for the care and maintenance of the kids and for the lion's share of the housework. The physical and emotional work of maintaining families, especially those with young children (and I don't have to tell you that kids require years and years of almost constant supervision and attention), is very demanding, but it is only just beginning to be appreciated by the lawmakers in our government and by American society in general.

Our government and some big businesses are already taking some steps to help, and other steps are still in the discussion stage: for example, maternity and paternity leave, child care subsidies or tax credits, extra tax deductions for families with children, and the overall quality of education have all been recently the focus of a lot of public debate and discussion. There are also signs of a new creature known as the "working father." These are men that are just as deeply involved with their children as mothers have always been. We even hear about more and more "househusbands" or "Mr. Moms." However, these cases are the exception to the rule, and still pretty rare.

Studies have also shown that modern women are remarkably resistant to giving up control of the caretaking role in families. Even though women's work in the home has always been demeaned ("Oh, I'm just a housewife") the home has always been where the woman ruled the roost, and where woman traditionally had a great deal of power, some perceived social value, and most importantly for the woman herself, a sense of satisfaction. I love my domain!

Don't ever forget that the whole idea of middle class families that have a stay-at-home Mom is actually a relatively new idea. The only route to economic survival for many 19th-century working-class families in America, for example, was to send their children into the mills and mines as early as age 7 or 8. So, if both the Mom and Dad are out working hard to keep a roof over the kid's heads it's definitely better than sending the kids out as child laborers!

What's the take-away here? How are we supposed to feel about this? For Neal and me, we were fortunate enough that I was able to make a choice to stay at home with the kids and "put my career on hold." I know this is not the case for most families today. And Neal was working so hard making money that he often didn't have the time or energy to contribute emotionally at home as much as he would have liked to. All these parents working so hard to provide food and shelter for their kids often don't have the energy to put in as much time as they would like to on the homefront – which is just one more reason that the concept of structured family dinners and family meetings are so much more important today than they ever were before. It is a simple idea with a whole lot of value, and talk about making the best use of time!

## So What is the Perfect Family?

**QUOTES**

In 1960, only nine percent of children under age 18 lived in single-parent homes. By 1999, the percentage rose to 27 percent. Today only 68 percent of children live in two-parent households, in contrast to 77 percent in 1980. Increases in divorce and out-of-wedlock births are responsible for this trend.

Stephanie Sado and Angela Bayer of
the Population Resource Center

It's becoming more and more obvious that there is no "perfect" family, and that Americans are choosing their own family structures. And while I may not agree that your idea of a perfect family structure is the right one, you may not agree that my idea of a perfect family structure is the right one. And since we're all lucky enough to live in a free country, we all have the ability to decide which the perfect family structure for our individual families is… and if we take the time to work on it, we can all find the inner strength to make whatever structure has been thrust upon us work as a family too.

So just what is a family these days? I guess it's whatever you decide your family is, whether that means a Mom and a Dad and two kids, or one Mom and some kids, or one Dad and some kids, or even grandparents and some kids, or any combination of adults and kids. We worked with a teen shelter over the past couple of years where the adult counselors took on the parent role. *If you call it your family then it's your family.*

> Female-headed households grew nearly five times faster than married-couple households with children in the 1990s.
> While married-couple households increased by fewer than six percent, female-headed households grew by 25 percent and the recent phenomenon of single-father households increased by 62 percent.
>
> Stephanie Sado and Angela Bayer<br>the Population Resource Center

**QUOTES**

So now that we've all agreed that families come in all shapes and sizes, here are some descriptions of families that hit home with me:

> Families are a set of primary relationships - biological, emotional, social, economic, and legal. Families are also a collection of individuals with differing needs and concerns living in complicated relationships with each other and with society. Families generally are expected to provide their members mutual economic, physical, and emotional support, meeting the human needs for food, shelter, and intimacy. Families also carry on tradition and culture and, in some instances, pass on property to the next generation.
>
> Arvonne S. Fraser

**TOGETHER**

**QUOTES**

> Family is lifelong *connectedness* and *accountability*. For better or worse, richer or poorer, in sickness and health, family is the place where we are *always* connected. And because of that, family is where we are *always* accountable. While we may hope that forgiveness will soften the pain, family is where we must live with our own and each other's mistakes. Bad marriages, failed businesses, and careless destruction of property or life – all these are family matters. In family we can't escape these things by moving away or declaring bankruptcy. We live till we die in the beds we make every day. So family is where we learn to be responsible, to put away our toys, clean up our messes, curb our violence and express our love.
>
> from *The Essence Of Family* by Vicki Robin

> Family is being there for each other. It is listening to one another, sharing with one another and supporting one another. It is having people to laugh with and to cry with. It is sharing and making memories and traditions. A family is all about unconditional love.
>
> from The Kimball family

# But My Family is Just So Different

### Defining Roles in the Family

Through choice or through no fault of their own, people find themselves in all sorts of families. And whether your current family structure is a result of marriage or divorce, choice or catastrophe, your family, like all individual families, deserves to be treated with respect. Despite the fact that we know that, single parents also know that children need a mother and a father and these single parents often feel called upon to try to play both roles.

> As far back as our knowledge takes us, human beings have lived in families. We know of no period where this was not so. We know of no people who have succeeded for long in dissolving the family or displacing it… Again and again, in spite of proposals for change and actual experiments, human societies have reaffirmed their dependence on the family as the basic unit of human living-the family of father, mother and children.
>
> From *Family* by Margaret Mead

**REMEMBER**

The problem here is that people know intuitively that the family has a standard form, a structure that is grounded in nature just by the simple fact that it takes a man and a woman to create a baby. Dutch historian Jan Romein termed the family "the common human pattern." Even when people consciously reject or bypass the traditional configuration of Mom, Dad and the kids, for whatever reasons, people tend to follow its patterns anyway, as if the family were a groove from which humanity cannot escape even when it tries to.

**WARNING**

Just try and figure out what roles the people that make up your family are going to play. Some families may have a female in the traditional Daddy role, or a male in the traditional Mommy role. Don't sweat it – whatever works for *your* family is best for *your* family.

# Chapter Three

# Chapter Four
# What Do You Want Out of This Experience?

## What Do You Want?

> "Nobody said it was going to be easy, but it's a commitment
> that you made when you became a parent... when you got
> involved with young people you made that commitment and
> it's one that you have to carry through with. It's not easy for
> kids these days either. Their role is quite difficult and often the
> choices that they face are life and death choices, much different
> from those that many of us faced when we were growing up.
> So it's not easy for anybody, but we have made a commitment
> and we need to follow through."
>
> Roxane Gilmore, First Lady of Virginia (1999)

**QUOTES**

The first question you need to ask yourself is just why are you reading
this book? The obvious answer is that you feel there is something either
lacking in your family structure, or in the way your family relates to
each other. Or perhaps you feel the way your family members relate to
the outside world could stand some improvement. Maybe it's a
combination of all three of those factors, or maybe it's just a vague
feeling of dissatisfaction with the way your family is turning out. Or
maybe you're very happy with the way that things are turning out and
you just want to make sure you're keeping an eye on things closely
enough along the way. Maybe you're just starting your family and want
to learn about things like family dinners and meetings right away.

**REMEMBER**

*Some of you reading this book may not technically be the "parents" of the kids that you'll be sitting down to the family table with. But, since you're reading this book, you're obviously assuming the "parental" role. In the interest of steering clear of confusing terms like " primary caregiver" I've chosen just to use the term "parent" to denote any adult who feels responsibility for the child or children in their (his or hers, or any combination thereof) care. This is just a simple, easy-to-understand term and nothing more.*

Neal and I like to use the analogy of our kids crossing over a bridge from youth to adulthood. As parents, we are supplying the guard rails so they don't fall off the bridge. During their youth, they may bump into the guard rails but with the right guidance, they will get back on track. As they cross over to the other side and leave the bridge and the guard rails behind, hopefully the modeling provided earlier on will keep them on the right path.

Always remember that if your family atmosphere is not anywhere near where you want it to be, you can change it! This is one of the reasons you're taking time out of your hectic schedule to read this book. If things aren't going so well, just keep reminding yourself that you are not stuck in the past, and you can always work on changing the future.

Although it is entirely natural for you to consciously or subconsciously recreate a family atmosphere similar to the one you grew up in, once you are able to calmly and rationally pick out things that you like and don't like about the family you grew up in, you might just decide to change some things. But change takes time, so be prepared to think about your goals and objectives for a little while until you decide to try and put them into action.

# Setting Goals and Objectives

If you don't have some goals or objectives regarding this whole family meal and meeting idea, it's unlikely that you will achieve the full benefit of the time you're planning on investing here.

So… what are your goals and objectives? What do you hope to achieve when you sit down and begin to have family meals and meetings? Please remember to always keep your goals achievable, so you don't get yourself discouraged if you find that you're not hitting all your goals in the first few months. Here are a few starter goals; some things you can think about while formulating your own goals and objectives:

**MEAL TIME**

## Family Meal and Meeting "Starter" Goals

✔ Make family meals a goal, but meet at least once a week, no matter what schedules we have to shift around to do it.

✔ Turn off the TV during meal times. Don't answer the phone either.

✔ Put someone in charge for the weekly family meal and meeting. Let them pick out the food and run the meeting.

✔ Everybody will actually contribute to the conversation.

✔ Everybody will help in either preparing the meal, setting the table, clearing the table or doing the dishes.

✔ This is not a chore! This is going to be fun!

✔ After we get going, we'll invite members of our extended family too.

As you can see, these are not long-term goals like "I want to open up clear lines of open and honest communication between all my family members." These are only short-term goals that will help you achieve your long-term goals. What those long-term goals may be for your family, I can't say – they will probably differ a little bit from family to family, depending on what your family's particular needs are. And only you, together with your family, can decide exactly what you want to take out of this whole experience.

Our family's short term goals were to relax for that one hour each day and regroup as a family. We wanted to see each others faces around the table, hear about our days and laugh with each other. Our long term goal is to connect now and in the future as a family that is always there for each other.

## What Do You Want Your Kids to Get out of This Experience?

**QUOTES**

"We all need transparent communication. Our relationships and our mental health depend upon transparent communication. We all must say what we mean in a way that is clear, understandable, kind and accurate. We want our children to be good communicators. We know that their communication skills will determine the success and quality of their relationships and of their works. They can best learn those skills at our knee, from the examples of our well-considered oral and body language, our integrity and our optimism."

Gayle Peterson, PhD, The Association
for Marriage and Family Therapy

I think one of the main reasons that Neal and I advocate family meals and meetings, beyond the idea of reconnecting with the family on a regular basis, is to lay the groundwork for a lifetime of clearer communication with our kids. What begins at the family table will hopefully spread out into all aspects of your children's lives.

Once your children get used to the idea that, no matter what, they're going to sit down at the table at least once a week and have a real conversation with their parents they might actually grow to *like* the idea. I know that our kids did.

Although I said earlier that only you could pick out your families goals and objectives, I think the over-riding objective for your kids here is clear – and that is creating clear lines of communication. Any other subsequent benefit we talk about here in this book, ranging the whole gamut from good table manners to using good judgment when thinking about premarital sex or teenage drug abuse, stems from having open and honest communication with your kids. Because if you're not communicating with your kids, you're certainly not going to be able to deliver any moral and philosophical messages that you might want to.

So, first and foremost, I think we can safely say that the first benefit that we want our kids to derive from the whole family dinner and meeting experience is opening up clear lines of communication between kids and parents.

# Why are We Doing This? Most People Already Eat Dinner Together, Don't They?

**QUOTES**

"We parents are the first and most important teachers of our children and teens. We must accept this fact as a personal challenge to our creative nature and to our intent. Our children will thrive in direct proportion to how reliably they can count on having a parent available when they need to talk, when they want inputs, when they want a hug communicating that they are loved or when they need assurance that life will work out. Our communication skills and our intentions will be of the greatest importance to our children in their work of creating themselves."

Gayle Peterson, PhD, The Association
for Marriage and Family Therapy

Picture a child sitting with a plate on his lap, watching a television program. You've seen it countless times, probably in your own house. Would it surprise you to know that many families do not even have a family table? Lots of people don't even know they're supposed to have tables! They weren't raised with them, they all ate their meals around the TV, and so they don't necessarily know how to have a dinner conversation. So, in an increasing number of households across America there is no dinnertime discussion going on, no sharing of family history, or of what happened that day at school and work – no communication passing between family members.

In America, many of us somehow assume that the idea of sitting around a table is genetically encoded. That probably came from us watching sitcoms of TV families sitting around the dinner table! Still there seems to be something so elemental in a table, so stable, so basic to our culture. But no, it's not an instinctive behavior, it really is a learned behavior, and many of us didn't learn it, and because of this we find it easier to watch a sitcom than to actually talk to our own family. Even with the whole family gathered around the dinner table, it can be difficult for parents who haven't taken the time to read a book like this to know what to say.

What we need to realize is that culture can be formed over a meal at the family table. Eating and connecting at the table is where an understanding of who we are, where we've been, and where we're going is transmitted. And especially for children, language is learned at the family table.

# Speak Up! They'll be Listening...

Just by the very nature of being children, our kids are inexperienced; they desperately need us to share experiences and feelings with them. Even if they seem resistant on the outside, they are hungry for our stories, because our stories help them define who they are and where they come from. Family stories told around a table help kids to create a personal history for themselves, and they also help to put things in perspective for a child. The more personal and family stories you tell around the table – no matter how silly or inconsequential they may seem to you – the more your kids will get used to listening to you.

My parents shared so much of their youth during our family meals around the table. Today, Neal and I love sharing our stories as kids with our children but we also continue to share our parent's stories. This is how cultures and traditions are passed down. The end result is that if we tell our ideas and stories with honesty and humor, maybe the kids will still be listening when we slip in some morals and philosophical advice for living!

# Helping Children Make Healthy Choices

**TOGETHER**

> "When it comes to alcohol and other important social issues, teaching children to make responsible decisions should begin at a young age – as early as eight or nine – and should continue throughout middle school, high school, and as they prepare for college. By giving young people the facts and helping them make the right decisions, we not only help fight underage drinking, but we underscore the importance of personal responsibility in the many choices children will make, especially if they choose to drink as adults."
>
> Dr. Lonnie Carton, director of Family Support
> Services for Boston Partners in Education

Through the increased communication we've been talking about in this chapter, we can find opportunities to help our kids make healthier choices. And I'm not just talking about health in the narrow sense of vitamins, good eating habits and physical exercise – although those are all certainly important. What I'm talking about here is overall health, the physical and mental well-being of our children.

I once heard a speaker talk about telling her kids about the importance of not having sex before marriage. Her kids would say every time she went into her *speech*, "We know Mom, not this speech again." And I loved her response… she said… "How many times do I ask you before bed if you brushed your teeth and your answer is I forgot?"

When errors in judgment are made by your kids, other family members can seek to help produce change through genuine warmth in communication, rather than just telling the child that they were flat out wrong. This does not mean that clear and defined punishments or consequences should not be forthcoming. Your child should always know that they will be held responsible for their actions. What it does mean, is that the motives or reasons behind the error in judgment should be looked at from a variety of different angles, rather than instantly assuming that the child in question was "bad" or "stupid."

We had a situation where one of our kids stole some gum from the grocery store. We went back to the store (I spoke to the manager beforehand), and had my six year old return it along with an apology. It was a tough consequence for him. The whole experience was discussed at our family meeting and all the kids learned from it. There was a consequence, he is still loved, and we all moved on! (PS: The manager was great, "I won't call the police this time but if it happens again…" It didn't!)

With the increased and clear communication that we've been talking about, one of the natural outcomes of this is that family members will believe in the inherent "goodness" of one another. When you're sitting down and talking on a regular basis, it should become natural to never assume bad intentions of each other.

Once you realize that an error in judgment is just that – an error – you can help correct future errors by guiding family meetings into discussions regarding hypothetical situations that your children may find themselves in. By discussing different reactions to different situations, and pointing out the merits or faults in all the reactions discussed, you'll be giving your kids a great grounding in decisions-making, and you'll be enabling them to make healthier choices all throughout their lives.

Listen, we're just getting our feet wet on this particular topic together. This is a tough one to jump right into, but I just wanted to bring this up now while we're still thinking about the sort of things we all want out of this whole family dinner and meeting experience. We'll talk about just how to guide these sorts of discussions on specific topics in chapters seven through twelve of this book, and I'll give you specific pointers on what to do to make these sorts of discussions positive and helpful for all involved.

# The Four Stable Legs
# of the Family Table

This is all starting to sound like a lot of stuff to be putting on one little old family dinner table doesn't it? Well, Neal and I have come up with some ideas that help to prop up the table and make it a rock-solid base for you to dump all those goals and objectives and hopes and dreams on.

For any family table to stand on its own, it needs to have four solid legs. These legs are built on some solid family-building principles that we've identified. You'll be able to see that you've probably got a lot of the things that work together to make strong legs in place already. Of course, some of the legs on your family table will be stronger than other legs... so these are the legs that you'll need to put most of the weight on as you build up all the other legs, until each leg of the table is able to bear the weight of the goals and objectives that you will soon be heaping onto the table.

We've identified the four legs of the family table as follows: **Social**, **Spiritual**, **Self-Sufficiency**, and **Learning**. After you read through this, you might want to think about how these legs relate to the goals and objectives you'll be setting for your family, and the subjects of discussion you might want to include in your family dinners and meetings.

# Social Leg

✔ **Connectedness and relationships:** A sense of connection between all members of the family, and a clear understanding of the relationships involved. Remember that parents need to be parents and kids need to be kids!

**IDEA**

✔ **Communication:** Well, I know this is almost the whole enchilada here in one bullet point, but it's included because none of this makes any sense without communication.

✔ **Family time:** There must be time that is set aside for you all to just be a family, and this is one of the major points of the whole family dinners and meetings idea.

✔ **Parental involvement:** You can't expect the kids to buy into any of this if you're not completely involved in the whole process, from beginning to end (and it never ends!)

✔ **Personal responsibility:** Instill the idea that although you face things as a family, everybody is ultimately responsible for their own actions.

✔ **Safety:** Kids and parents alike should know that although risk-taking is an essential part of any growing experience, risks should be more based in emotional and social factors than in situations where you're actually putting life and limb in danger. Safety also means that kids should never have to fear unreasonable reactions from their parents in any situation.

✔ **Building trust:** All family members should know that they won't get blasted for bringing up a subject for conversation – they need to be able to trust that you will engage in open and honest dialogue. Building trust also means that they should be able to rely on the fact that their family is a safety net that will always be there to catch them when they stumble a little bit as they make their way through life. Trust is stronger than fear.

✔ **Substance abuse awareness:** To prevent your kids from stumbling too hard, you need to make them aware of the dangers of drugs early and often. This can't be stressed hard enough. And don't leave out the socially acceptable drugs like tobacco and alcohol – these can and do kill just as surely as heroin.

✔ **Guardianship:** You must always remember that you, as a parent (and remember what I said about who parents are at the beginning if the chapter) have a sacred trust. You are your kid's guardian in every sense of the word!

## Spiritual Leg

**IDEA**

✔ **Faith:** Although Neal and I have dedicated our family to a certain faith, we wouldn't want to suggest that there is one true faith for all families. What we would like to stress is that it is important that you offer your children some sort of faith. Whatever it is you believe in, from Christianity to Zen Buddhism to secular humanism, it's very important that you give your children an opportunity to develop that faith for themselves.

✔ **Study of Faith:** Don't leave the instruction of your kids in your chosen faith to the "professionals" in that field. Your faith should be a living, breathing thing, and the kids should get the chance to dissect it in family conversations. You certainly don't need to be an expert; you just need to tell your kids what you believe in and why. You might just be a little surprised how much stronger your faith becomes when you're forced to explain it in simple term to an inquisitive five year-old!

# Self-Sufficiency Leg

✔ **Healthy eating/nutrition:** While you have your kids at the table, you have the opportunity to teach them good nutritional habits. Don't just tell them carrots and vegetables are good for them – explain how it will help them get bigger and stronger. You may need to do a little further reading on this one!

**IDEA**

✔ **Physical wellness:** This ties into the nutrition bullet point – while you're getting your kids to eat the carrots, explain to them how a little exercise and a little fresh air will go a long way to keeping them happier and healthier.

✔ **Emotionally stable:** By discussing *any* topic with honesty and empathy, you'll be able to keep your kids from getting too freaked out about things, and keep them on a more even keel when they're faced with potentially upsetting events.

✔ **Financial understanding:** Just like substance abuse awareness, kids can't hear about finances too early or too often. I don't mean you need to explain how much it hurts to pay the rent or mortgage every month, I mean that kids should understand the fact that it takes time and effort to make the money necessary to put food on the table, clothes on their back and toys in their room. If they understand the value of money early, it may help them stay out of money trouble later.

✔ **Self-determination:** Let your kids know that nothing in life is pre-determined. We live in America, and that means that every one of us has the right and obligation to try and be the best person we can be. Your children should know that while your family will always be there to help them, it's truly up to them what kind of person they will be.

✔ **Authority and freedom:** This is a tough one to balance. While you should instill in your kids that everyone is "free to be you and me" you should also let them know that you are the ultimate authority in your family, and sometimes the discussion is over!

## Learning Leg

**IDEA**

✔ **Reading literacy:** Obviously, you can read. It's a national tragedy just how many Americans in this day and age cannot. Get books in your kid's hands at an early age, and let them see you reading too. Reading habits learned early can have a serious influence on a child's learning and earning capabilities throughout their lives.

✔ **Homework time/help:** Set aside a specific time every night for your kids to do their homework, and be available to help them when they get stuck. They'll have homework almost every night – it's actually kind of wild how much homework kids get these days, I don't seem to remember getting that much homework in grammar school. But, your kids are getting homework now, for sure, and you need to make sure that they're doing it!

✔ **Parenting education:** Hey, you already have this one covered. You're engaged in parenting education right now! But education is a continual process... so remember to keep an open mind as you move forward.

# Set Your Goals and Objectives

Okay, by now you've got an idea about how to go about setting realistic
goals and objectives for your family dinners and meetings experience.
Keep the things you've read in this chapter in mind while you're
thinking about what you want this exercise to bring to your family
table. And while I know that the list of the elements that make up the
legs of the family table may seem daunting, you'll see that you can
work towards improving all those areas of your family life if you don't
take on too many tasks at one time.  Let your family help you set your
goals, remember to make your goals achievable, and take small steps
towards building the four stable legs of your family table.

**REMEMBER**

# Chapter Four

# Chapter Five
## Reclaiming Time

## Don't Make Time – Reclaim it

In his book *If I Were Starting My Family Again*, John Drescher wrote about a study of 300 seventh and eighth-grade boys who kept detailed records of how much time their fathers spent with them over a two-week period. Most saw their father only at the dinner table. A number didn't see their fathers for days at a time. The average time father and son were alone together was seven and one-half minutes a week.

Gospel Communication International

**QUOTES**

There's only a certain amount of time in the day when you're actually at home and have the ability to be available to your children. We all have work to do, errands to run and chores to complete. A lot of parents console themselves on the amount of time they spend with their children by rationalizing that, "Although we don't spend a huge amount of time together, the time we do spend is quality time." Well, if the study by John Drescher is true, then it seems to me that a lot of men spend more time per day with their razor than they do with their children. If that seven and a half minute figure is correct, then we all may need to reexamine our priorities. Do we really think we should spend more time shaving each week than we spend with our kids? Of course not.

In *Teens and Their Parents in the 21st Century: An Examination of Trends in Teen Behavior and the Role of Parental Involvement,* the Council of Economic Advisors indicated that active, consistent parental involvement is a major influence in helping youth avoid risky behaviors, such as drug use and early sexual activity. In addition, young people who have a close relationship with their parents are more likely to have higher grade point averages and go to college.

While I think that we should take a lot of studies with a grain of salt, there has to at least be some truth in the supposition that we're not spending enough time with our kids. If not, professionals wouldn't even bother to fund studies looking into the problem.

**So what should we do?  What would "quality time" include?**

As hard as this may be to admit, I think most of you will agree with me that the whole concept of quality time is just a rationalization that people use to escape creeping feelings of guilt that they might not be spending enough time with their kids.  And I think that if you really look at it, you'll see that the concept of quality time just doesn't stand up unless you're actually talking about a *quantity* of time as well.

Here are some other ways we justify not spending enough time with our kids, (and I'll poke holes in them too):

**WARNING**

> "My kids are still really young, so if I'm not around so much for the first couple of years, it won't matter that much."

Well, if that's what you're thinking then you're going to end up missing a lot.  Lots of things only happen once in a child's life, like the day they learn how to walk backwards and spend the next few days backing around the house and giggling when they bump into things!  It seems so simple that sometimes we forget: toddlers do not remain toddlers for long.

> "They're still so young that they won't remember if I was here or not."

**WARNING**

### Don't bet on that!

Kids form emotional bonds early on, and it can flavor their relationships for the rest of their lives. By the same token, if you come into a child's life at a later date – for example, by marrying someone who already has toddlers – don't think it's too late for you to make an impact. The old Greeks knew what they were talking about when they advised us to "Carpe Diem!" You need to "seize the day" and take advantage of every opportunity you have to be with your children. Nobody really knows which moments are going to be locked forever into a child's memory. Just think about some of your earliest memories. They seem pretty random, don't they? And not even the best child psychiatrists can pinpoint exactly which experiences will mark turning points in a child's life.

A child's behavioral development is established at an earlier age than you may think. And even if you may not be able to remember specific moments of your early childhood, you do have sense memories from that age. A sense of well-being and love during this time in a child's development is crucial, because that feeling of togetherness will be remembered later.

> "I'll make it up to them later, because I have plenty of time. I'll concentrate on my career now so that when they're older so we'll have plenty of money to spend on activities we all enjoy."

**WARNING**

This common thought is sadly wrong on so many levels. First off, nobody can predict what tomorrow will bring. To quote a familiar phrase, "You could get hit by a bus tomorrow." Do you think that all those people in Washington DC and New York City thought that September 11, 2001 was going to be any different than any other day in their lives? Now, it may seem a little harsh to think of it in these terms, but nobody is guaranteed a long life.

Secondly, do you really believe that you'll have more free time in a few years? Busy lifestyles don't change when we reach a certain age; they just become more deeply ingrained. The better that you get at your job, the more promotions you'll receive and the more time you'll be expected to put in at your job to fulfill your mounting career responsibilities. Nobody gets more than twenty-four hours in a day and what you choose to do with those hours can tell you a lot about what is really important to you.

Lastly, to borrow from another familiar phrase, if you're "saving for a rainy day," then you need to realize something. When it comes to not spending time with your family – it's already raining!

## But Where Will We Get the Time?

QUOTES

> "Effective family life does not just happen. It's the result of deliberate intention, determination, and practice."
> Barbara Glanz, *Care Packages for the Home*

To put it quite simply, you don't need to make time – reclaim it. Set time aside to eat and really *talk* with your family. Spending your meals parked on the couch in silence, while the family watches what's on television isn't "quality" time.

I know that we all have responsibilities outside of the home. Times are changing, roles are getting wider and harder to fulfill, but you can insure that family dinners and meetings are here to stay. They may be microwaveable, or store-bought "home replacement" meals – you might not be cooking away like Betty Crocker or Aunt Jemima – but you can take the time and effort to make sure that you all sit down at the table together, at least once a week.

You might ask, "Why meal time?" The reason is that meals provide an opportunity for a family to spend time together. Around a table, we sit facing one another. We can converse and find out about each other's day and what is happening tomorrow. Families are on the "expressway" of life, and we are speeding along, not taking the time for a break. It's important to take the scenic tour once in a while—to stop and take it all in. It's time to let go of the day – to stop, unwind, and *talk*.

When we first tested our idea in our own family, we made a commitment to have at least one meal together each week. We felt this was realistic and "do-able." However, we had to be flexible about the actual dinner hour. It often meant waiting until 7:30 at night to eat, if that was the only time that would work. Sometimes we would gather for Sunday brunch!

**EXAMPLE**

## Tips For Reclaiming Time

✔ **Make quick and easy dinners.**

✔ **Ask your friends for recipes you can throw together in fifteen minutes.**

✔ **Buy pre-cut or pre-prepared meat and vegetables at the grocery store.**

✔ **Plan ahead by making extra food one night and serving the same meal, or a variation of it, later in the week.**

✔ **If dinner time is just too hectic, try breakfast, lunch or Sunday brunch.**

And while I'm talking about time and effort, I don't mean that having a family dinner and meeting should be a chore for everyone involved, instead you should try and make it fun for the whole crew. So, while this whole effort may begin with you dragging the kids away from the TV with much weeping and wailing and kicking and screaming, eventually you'll come to realize that it's actually fun to sit down at a table together – as a family.

**TOGETHER**

> In one month I'll be a teenager – and I think that most teenagers have a hard time talking to their families and parents – and I don't – we have a huge line of communication. I take the time to talk with my family and I love to know what's going on and when – and so with the meetings I feel a part and know what's going on and can also say what's on my mind and express myself.
>
> Maggie Kimball (my daughter!)

Our older children are just entering their teen years. These years are frightening for most parents, but we are entering them with confidence because we have made our family a priority through eating meals together, especially at dinnertime. Whatever issues come up, we know that we will face them with a strong foundation of communication and trust with our children. I thank God every night that we made the decision four years ago to begin to change our schedules and make family time a priority! We know that we only have a few years left with all of us together in the home, and we are going to value this time.

**Here are some different ways you can make your family dinners and meetings fun. Some of these may require "props" like certain books, or art supplies:**

**IDEA**

✔ Send a local postcard to a far away friend

✔ Ask your child's opinions

✔ Take pictures of your family

✔ Help your child find your city on a map

✔ Help your child trace their hand on a paper

✔ Share special family memories

✔ Sing songs together

✔ Talk to your children about family rules and why they are needed

✔ Hug anyone

✔ Have lollipops for dessert

✔ Talk about how can you make the world a better place

✔ Think up 10 special things about your family

✔ Read the newspaper together

✔ Give your child an "I like it when..." note

✔ Call a relative and let everyone talk on the phone

**IDEA**

✔ Surprise an old friend with a phone call

✔ Write a family letter to someone you all like

✔ Share a meal with another family

✔ Sing

✔ Look for signs of the new season coming

✔ Have everyone learn a joke, and then have everyone tell their joke

✔ Eat dessert first today

✔ List all the good things you and your kids do

✔ Look for bird nests

✔ Talk about what it means when we say we are a global village

✔ Make a list of deceased loved ones, and think up special memories of each one

✔ Look at pictures in your old photo albums

✔ Life is 10% what happens to me and 90% how I react

✔ Read a favorite poem

✔ Plan a meal prayer

✔ Rekindle an old friendship

- ✔ Eat an ethnic food meal

- ✔ I'm sorry for...

- ✔ Exchange roles in the family for one meal

- ✔ Trade chores

- ✔ No negative comments!

- ✔ Take a different seat at the dinner table

- ✔ Take flowers to the cemetery

- ✔ Wear a blindfold for an hour – this one gets messy!

- ✔ Learn a card trick

- ✔ Do something that you have never done before

- ✔ Say your family name backwards, and then try everyone's first name backwards

- ✔ Have everyone make dinner

- ✔ Share the best news you have heard lately

- ✔ Share a tub of ice cream

- ✔ Decide which canned goods to donate to a food pantry

- ✔ Find out the meaning of your names

**IDEA**

See! The family dinner and meeting doesn't have to be a grim thing where you sit down and work through all of the perceived problems in your family. Be careful when you use these tips, you all might find out that you're actually enjoying yourselves!

# Involving the Kids in Dinner Planning

**TOGETHER**

> I told a friend of mine about it and he said, "Cool, I want to get my family to do it too," – so kids like it!
> Jimmy Kimball (my son!)

When Neal and I first began to have our once weekly planned family sit-down dinner and meeting, we tried to come up with ways to get the kids more involved in the whole process. We decided that we would have a different Kimball family member appointed weekly to conduct the meeting and choose the dinner menu each week.

Of course, when the younger kids got to choose the family menu we had some pretty bizarre items on the dinner table, but we had committed to the idea so we suffered through a few odd dinners. However, you should always remember that you're supposed to be the adult in this whole scenario, so feel free to make the kids choose again if they want chocolate cake and ice cream for dinner... although that doesn't sound too bad right about now!

You can set guidelines for the kids: for example, tell them that they must include at least one vegetable on the menu. Of course, you'll set guidelines according to what you feel should be included in every meal. Some families never sit down without some potatoes on the table; some families must have rice or bread. It all depends on the particular family, but once the kids know the rules it will be easier for everyone involved!

# You Know, You Don't Even Have to Cook!

Family meals at restaurants are memorable and break up the monotony of cooking. To save money, use coupons or, if possible, hit the "early bird" specials. It really doesn't matter if you cooked the meal or not, as long as you are together as a family. We need this time with our children. National studies have found that the more often a child eats dinner with his or her parents, the less likely that child is to smoke, drink, or use drugs. Another survey found that strong families structure their schedules so that spending time becomes a regular part of their life. And that's what we're asking you to do – hopefully, the suggestions in this chapter have made it easier for your to see your way clear to scheduling weekly family dinners and meetings.

# A Date We Never Break

After recognizing the value and fun of regular family meals, we now eat together as often as we can. We also continue to have a family meeting once a week. We have made our dinner table a "safe zone," where feelings can be shared, thoughts can be communicated openly and honestly, and where everyone is valued and heard. It is a fun and relaxing experience – something our kids look forward to and enjoy.

**REMEMBER**

The nineteen families in our test group experienced so much success with implementing our idea that they urged us to spread the word. It's one more reason why we're getting so evangelical about something that should really just be a part of normal American family life, but has become a part of old family tradition that was slipping away with the times. What used to be so ordinary and natural in families – eating meals together – is becoming less and less of a reality, so Neal and I hope that this book can help families put their desire for regular meal times into practice.

# There is a Payoff!

Four years ago, Neal and I faced the reality that strong families don't just "happen." We had to make our family life a priority. Even in these few short years, we have seen several "payoffs" from our investment in family time. The fruit is open and honest relationships, where values are shared and taught and where respect and love for each other can grow.

For example, we have become kinder, not only to one another but to those outside the home as well. Here are some solid examples of the benefits we've received from eating dinner together as a family:

✔ A cafeteria worker told our daughter recently that she was the only student who said "thank you" when she returned her tray to the dishwasher area.

✔ We often receive compliments about how polite and considerate our children are.

✔ Our children not only have stronger relationships with us but with each other. They actually enjoy each other's company and are anxious to help one another.

✔ Our oldest child told us that she was faced with a choice recently about whether to participate in some questionable behavior with her peers at school. However, she thought about our family mission statement, and it helped her to say "no" to her friends.

Perhaps most important of all is that we truly have a lot of fun together. Our kids *want* to be home and spend time as a family. That's more than worth making the time and effort to gather the family around and sit down to a meal as often as possible!

Simple prioritization is the key that you can and should use to unlock the door to a better family. And once you sit down together as a family and make the tough decisions, things will begin to improve. It may not happen overnight, and there may be bumps along the way. But if you persevere, then it can and will be done.

Chapter Five

# Chapter Six
# Dynamics of Family Communication

## Good Communication

> "Good communication requires willingness to listen and respond, to give and receive, and to acknowledge what is being communicated without manipulating, limiting or denying reality. Good communication is the ability to openly express one's own feelings and thoughts without judgment. Good communication is respectful of all concerned. Communication includes not only words, but also facial expression, intonation, volume, touch, and body movement."
>
> Deb Gebeke, Family Science Specialist,
> Kim Bushaw, Parent Line Program Specialist,
> *in Family Communication and Family Meetings*

**QUOTES**

The essential element of the family dinners and meetings that Neal and I hold with our children is *communication*. It doesn't matter whether we're sitting down to a Sunday brunch or a take-out pizza, as long as we're communicating as a family and on meeting nights we have a specific agenda that outlines what we want to talk about; then we're having a family dinner and meeting. None of the external trappings matter if real communication doesn't occur.

One way to ensure clear communication is to always strive to talk *with* your kids and not *to* your kids. There's a very subtle difference between the two. While sometimes you have to be the parent and put your foot down, at other times you really need to discuss why something is occurring.

We have found that a lot of parents use examples from their childhoods to make a case for why something should be done or why something is not that hard to do. Parents find themselves saying things like, "When I was your age, my parents would never let me do that!" or using examples like "I used to get up every morning and do an hour of chores before I went to school." We joke about hearing stories from our parents like. "I used to walk four miles to school in two feet of snow, up hill both ways," but then we end up using less ridiculous but similar tactics when we discuss things with our kids!

Well, guess what? Just like it didn't work with you... that sort of communication won't work with your kids either! It's just about impossible for kids to relate to this sort of history. Their reaction is likely to be boredom, which will result in them shutting you out, rather than giving any serious thought to what it was like when you were growing up. I do believe, however, that sometimes relating a story that happened to me that taught me a lesson is a great way to share a lesson. It doesn't come off as preachy – rather it makes the kids think by letting them "hear" the outcome and then make a decision of how to use that knowledge for their circumstances.

# This is Going to Hurt Me More Than it Hurts You

"Even though my wife and I can think of times we wish we had said or done something differently with our two sons, we tried to do our best; we always cared. In looking back, we often think about how much we've learned. As parents, we're all givers and receivers… teachers and learners."

Fred Rogers, star of Mr. Rogers Neighborhood

**QUOTES**

**WARNING**

When you say things like, "I'm doing this for your own good" or "You'll thank me for this some day," you're just pumping the conversation full of words that have very little meaning to your kids. You're also talking down to them by assuming that they just can't understand whatever it is you were discussing.

But most importantly, you have shifted the focus of the discussion and avoided giving any reasons for what you are saying. If you have a rule in your house that the kids need to finish their chores and their homework before watching TV, just be clear about the rule and don't hide your reasoning behind clichéd expressions or stories of your ancient history. Just state your reasons plainly and try to be open to a rational discussion with your children.

In order to talk *with* your kids, and not *to* your kids, you need to explain exactly why a rule exists. If your children have an alternative to your rule, attempt to be open to trying their ideas for a certain period of time. Come to an agreement that you will all have another family meeting to discuss the rule in question and decide which way worked best. I remember when we got a trampoline for the back yard and our family's rule was only one person on at a time for safety reasons. About two weeks into having the trampoline, the kids came to us (at a family meeting – and they were very prepared, I might add) wanting to be able to have two on at a time. They shared with us that with the safety of the net it would be okay and we should try it out and revisit the rule at the next meeting. They sold us and we revised the rule with their input. And remember, never say, "I told you so," if you do end up going back to the original rule.

# Family Communication Theories and Styles

**WARNING**

"Not all family members communicate in the same manner or at the same level. This is especially true of young children. When communicating with young children, it is important for adults to listen carefully to what the children are saying without making unwarranted assumptions. It is also important to take into consideration the ages and maturity levels of children. Parents cannot communicate with children in the same way that they communicate with their spouse because the child may not be old enough to understand."

Rick Peterson, Assistant Professor,
Department of Human Development, Virginia Tech,
in Families *First-Keys to Successful Family Functioning: Communication*

There have been plenty of books written on this subject, and some doctors make an entire career out of examining family communication styles. I just want to go over this at the surface level, just so that everybody understands that there is more than one way to communicate in a family setting.

I've found that Connie Podesta, a professional counselor, talks about communication styles in her book *Life Would Be Easy If It Weren't for OTHER People*, in a very simple and understandable way:

Every time we speak, we choose and use one of four basic communication styles: assertive, aggressive, passive and passive-aggressive.

✔ **Assertive Communication**

The most effective and healthiest form of communication is the assertive style. It's how we naturally express ourselves when our self-esteem is intact, giving us the confidence to communicate without games and manipulation.

**EXAMPLE**

When we are being assertive, we work hard to create mutually satisfying solutions. We communicate our needs clearly and forthrightly. We care about the relationship and strive for a win/win situation. We know our limits and refuse to be pushed beyond them just because someone else wants or needs something from us. Surprisingly, assertive is the style most people use least.

✔ **Aggressive Communication**

Aggressive communication always involves manipulation. We may attempt to make people do what we want by inducing guilt (hurt) or by using intimidation and control tactics (anger). Covert or overt, we simply want our needs met – and right now! Although there are a few arenas where aggressive behavior is called for (i.e., sports or war), it will never work in a relationship. Ironically, the more aggressive sports rely heavily on team members and rational coaching strategies. Even war might be avoided if we could learn to be more assertive and negotiate to solve our problems.

✔ **Passive Communication**

Passive communication is based on compliance and hopes to avoid confrontation at all costs. In this mode we don't talk much, question even less, and actually do very little. We just don't want to rock the boat. Passives have learned that it is safer not to react and better to disappear than to stand up and be noticed.

✔ **Passive-Aggressive Communication**
A combination of styles, passive-aggressive avoids direct confrontation (passive), but attempts to get even through manipulation (aggressive). If you've ever thought about making that certain someone who needs to be "taught a thing or two" suffer (even just a teeny bit), you've stepped pretty close to the devious and sneaky world of the passive-aggressive.

Connie Podesta

Positioning your statements during communications is also very important, and it's very easy to do. We would always get asked why our kids are so positive, and it has a lot to do with positioning. For example, when we found out we were going to have to move again (one of our many moves!), our presentation would never be "Kids, we have some terrible news…" but instead, we would say "Kids, we have some very exciting news…" It never ceases to amaze me how many times parents take the negative approach in sharing news with their kids instead of the positive.

# Determining Which Style Works Best for My Family

After you read the above discussion of communication styles, it's obvious that you should choose to teach your family and yourself to communicate in the assertive style. You can do this by engaging in open and honest discussions with your kids whenever possible, and especially during family dinners and meetings. If your children are taught to approach their involvement in family discussions in an assertive style, then this most forthright of communication styles will most likely spill over into other portions of their lives. Sometimes we are amazed at the confidence our children have in their communication styles with people of all ages.

But if you really take a good look at yourself, you'll see that most of the time in communication you're using a combination of the four styles. And most people do use a combination of these four styles, depending on the person they're talking to or the situation they find themselves in. As a parent, you really need to concentrate on communicating in the assertive style if you want to have a chance of schooling your kids to communicate in this manner.

By understanding the four basic types of communication you'll be able to react more effectively when you find your kids using manipulative behaviors. Once you understand that your child is conversing in a passive-aggressive mode, for example, you'll then be able to direct the conversation in a more productive manner by responding in an assertive manner. Understanding these styles will also help you recognize when you are using manipulative behavior to get your own point across.

As an adult, you always have a choice as to which communication style you employ. I know you're serious about increasing family communication or you wouldn't be reading this book – now you need to move on to the next level and practice being more assertive in your everyday communications.

# Elements of Open and Honest Communication

When you're getting ready to begin your family dinners and meeting, there are some points you might want to remember to help encourage the assertive style of communication amongst your family members:

**IDEA**

✔ Everyone in the family should be included in the discussions.

✔ Everyone should be actively encouraged to participate so that nobody can ever say, "I didn't get a chance to talk." If somebody isn't communicating, then ask that person to join in. Everybody has an opinion, but sometimes they just need to be prompted to give it. Jimmy, at age 6, needed some prompting but really got into it after he was given the floor!

✔ Listen with an open mind; always remember that there is usually more than one way to solve a situation. We not only need to listen to children but we need to acknowledge that we have heard and understood what they said. This often includes thoughts that are not totally expressed by words alone. Body language and facial expressions also send powerful messages.

✔ One bad communication habit that many people have is that we are often so busy thinking of what we're going to say next we don't listen to what someone is actually saying to us. We anticipate what other family members are going to say and we end up interrupting them or reacting to what they are saying before they actually say it! This is even harder to avoid with very young children who can take a long time to put their thoughts into words.

Our natural impulse is to hurry them along, finish sentences for them or put words into their mouths. Fight that impulse! Let everyone have their say before you put in your own two cents! Our biggest problem is with all the kids"filler words" they use before they get to the point, the 'likes, ums, stuff, you know'. Neal and I have to be conscious not to finish their sentences for them! (We also are working on getting rid of those words in our own communications, too!)

✔ Tone of voice may provide a clear hint of the feelings that your children might be struggling to put into words. If you really listen to how they are saying something, in addition to what they are saying, you should be able to figure out if they are angry, happy, frustrated, enthusiastic, tired, full of energy, bored, or interested, even if they may not actually be vocalizing those feelings. Children also will pick up on your tone... sometimes we are careful about the *content* of what we are saying but forget that our *tone* can take away from the seriousness of what we are saying, intimidate our children, or fuel nasty arguments. Our own parents tried to teach us this when they said "Watch your tone!" or "Don't you take that tone with me!"

✔ Body language may give an additional clue to unexpressed feelings. Watch your children's facial expressions. Sometimes what they are doing with their hands can express what the person is feeling. How is the body positioned? Are they standing, sitting, reclining? Sharpening your observation skills may allow you to better understand those around you, and enable you to draw them out further into a healthy and assertive communication style. Also, remember that actions speak louder than words. It is important that your verbal and nonverbal messages match. For example, if you say something nice but your arms are folded and your facial expression looks angry, your compliment will be discounted. Likewise, if you smile and look playful while enforcing a rule, you won't be taken seriously. Remember to model clear, consistent communication.

✔ It's never a bad idea to take notes, so that things can be sorted out later. Sometimes the conversation will go off on a tangent that will show you that other ideas may need more thought. This approach will also feel a lot better than getting feedback that your idea is just irrelevant or off-topic and will be ignored.

✔ People are going to get angry, inevitably. When anger does crop up, you can always take a little time-out and hopefully come back to the table a little more willing to work through the challenges. You might want to say to your child, "I'm angry now. Our talk will go better if we discuss this after I calm down," or "Let's take a brief time-out and go to our own rooms to think about it and then we'll talk more." Temporarily separating yourself from the situation or the person is often an effective strategy to pave the way for a constructive, rational, calm discussion. We have a saying in our house, "Stop, Drop and Roll." We use it a little differently than with the fire warning, but it still has to do with heat! In our family, if we are getting into a heated discussion we say "Stop, drop and roll" and that tells us to separate and regroup later when we are calmer.

✔ Show that you have the ability to compromise. Rarely does anyone get to have his or her way all the time and on every point. Once your kids see that you're being reasonable on certain topics, they might just decide to be reasonable themselves. Also, if you have shown that you can bend in certain situations, they may be more willing to accept the fact that other situations are non-negotiable.

✔ Sometimes you can agree to disagree – obviously, this can't be done on matters that affect safety, morality or family ethics. And this must only be done when all family members do so with the full understanding that everybody can share values without necessarily sharing the same opinion.

✔ Common courtesy and civility must be insisted on at all times in family discussions. Rude and disruptive remarks should not be tolerated! We have some fair fighting rules posted on our refrigerator. Don't bring up past stuff, don't use the phrases "You never" or "You always", etc. Respect for everyone is the goal. Teaching how to respect individuals while disagreeing with their ideas is an important life skill.

✔ If you can't get through the topic in one meeting, then schedule another one! Sometimes ideas need to be explored and new facts presented before a final decision on some matter is made. Time can diffuse conflict.

✔ Sometimes you may need the help of an objective outside party. Many social workers are trained mediators and able to help families negotiate sensitive issues with a goal to having the best possible outcome. This should only be used in extreme cases, because you don't want your kids to get the idea they can call someone in to usurp your authority on a regular basis.

# What are Some General Guidelines for Effective Family Meetings?

I've read that some people believe you should only begin to have family meetings after your relationship with your children is one of mutual respect and honesty. I'm not sure I agree with that – I think family meetings can go a long way towards creating those feelings of mutual respect and honesty. And properly run family meetings may not be possible for your family at this very moment, but with an investment of time and effort you will soon be having family meetings in which everybody at the table is contributing in a positive and assertive manner. It is all about proper modeling. The outcome will pleasantly surprise you.

**TOGETHER**

Here are some slightly adapted guidelines for family meetings that Deb Gebeke, Family Science Specialist, and Kim Bushaw, Parent Line Program Specialist, laid down in their paper called *Family Communication and Family Meetings*.

✔ Establish a specific regular meeting time. Weekly is a good way to start.

✔ Take advantage of driving time to discuss issues when meetings are not possible. Sometimes car conversations are a gift, turn the radio off and talk and listen, you will be amazed!

✔ Establish and stick to time contracts.

✔ Make sure all members have a chance to offer ideas.

✔ Encourage everyone to bring up issues. Write them down, keep a list until the next meeting and discuss them in proper order.

✔ Don't permit meetings to become gripe sessions.

✔ Plan family fun to meet the interests of all ages.

✔ Use your communication skills. Listen with sensitivity, speak with respect for feelings and never use put-downs.

✔ Evaluate decisions at the next meeting.

✔ Don't use family meetings to attempt to solve one person's problems. Meetings are not therapy sessions. Use the meeting to share feelings and make suggestions. Seek professional help for problems.

✔ Even families with one child can benefit from family meetings. Decision-making is still important for everyone.

✔ Remember that parents are not the only ones in charge. No one person should have control over meetings. Take turns leading the meetings, and involve everyone in an age-appropriate way.

✔ Follow through on agreements. At the time agreements are made, build in logical consequences for broken agreements.

✔ All members participate in family meetings as equals.

These are only guidelines to help you start thinking about how to use your communication skills in a family meeting setting. Later on in the chapter, you'll read the specific steps Neal and I and the Dunns have come up with on how to run a successful family meeting.

# Sometimes You May Need to be a *Little* Aggressive

I realize that all this theory about open and honest discussion sometimes runs up against that brick wall we call "real life." As parents, we always have to remember that not everything is negotiable, and not everything is always on the table for discussion. You need to let the kids realize that certain rules are rules and that's that!

Specifically, when you set out rules regarding behaviors that are unsafe, your kids need to know there is no "wiggle" room. These rules could be as simple as always insisting they wear a helmet when they ride their bikes, or as profound as the all-encompassing "never take candy from strangers." Your kids need to know that if they break certain rules that there will be no discussion, and that the consequences will be immediate and unvarying. For example: If you ride your bike without a helmet, you will not be permitted to ride your bike again for the period of one week.

When we "draw the line" on a rule or discussion topic, we always have to make sure that we are consistent in the application of the consequences. Although this chapter is stressing the importance of open and honest communication, some rules laid down by the parents must be seen as non-negotiable. When you explain a particular non-negotiable rule to a child you should always tell them your reasons behind the rule, in the hope that they might see the wisdom behind it, but you should make it clear that certain rules are to be followed no matter what, and proceed from there. If a child does not understand the reasoning behind the rule, validate their frustration and confusion, try to clarify your explanation by using age appropriate examples or metaphors they may understand, and if they still don't understand let them know that sometimes children just have to trust their parents to protect them. Keep in mind that when you are helping them understand why you have set rules, you do not need to justify your right to do so!

# How to Begin Having Family Meals and Meetings

Now that we've discussed how different families may set different goals and objectives for their family meetings, why we want to have family meetings, and how to most constructively communicate during those meetings, it's time to actually begin having family meetings.

You need to schedule your family meetings well in advance of the actual date, as everyone's schedule can tend to be hectic (especially as your kids get older). Use your family calendar to discuss the upcoming week's schedule.

Family or individual practices, games, work schedules, parties, service projects, and commitments for the upcoming week should all be included on your family calendar. Communication at the beginning of each week will aid in keeping the family informed on the activities of each family member — allowing the week to run more smoothly. Our child, Maggie, is a "who, what, when, where" kind of person. Talking about the schedules for the upcoming week helps her tremendously. You can prioritize activities and ensure that important events are scheduled, to minimize surprises. You may have to adjust the family's meal schedule on different days of the upcoming week. With a little compromise and a lot of communication, you can ensure that everyone will sit down together when meal is served. *This is also a good time to schedule the next week's family meeting.*

# Here's How to Run a Family Meeting

## We start our weekly family meeting after the meal.

**EXAMPLE**

The **Leader** runs the weekly family meeting and keeps the meeting on track. Every family member should get the chance to be the Leader; every week there should be a new Leader. As the Leader, you get to decide on the dinner and dessert, and choose the **Talking Torch**. This is an object (a baseball card, a spoon, a picture, a stuffed animal, or something special to that week's Leader) that gives the holder the power to speak — uninterrupted — during your family meeting. When that person is finished speaking, the Talking Torch is passed on to someone else, and so on. In addition to ensuring that everyone has a turn to speak, this technique teaches listening skills and encourages taking turns.

The Leader also keeps the meeting moving and under control. A new Leader should be chosen each week. Tell everyone that this is a rotating position and that each person will have a turn at leading the meeting. While the dynamics of the meeting may change from week to week, depending on the leader – parent or child – all family members will feel a sense of involvement and belonging.

Begin your meetings with compliments for each family member. This not only sets the tone for a positive meeting, but also will help build your children's confidence and self-esteem. Have the **Leader** pass the **Talking Torch** around the table to each person in turn.

When you are holding the torch, it is your turn to compliment other family members, note their accomplishments, or mention their good deeds during the past week. This was hard for our kids in the beginning. Our kids didn't know how to compliment. We were hearing things like "You didn't tease me that bad this week," "When you hit me this week it wasn't as bad as last week." But as Neal and I showed how to compliment by example, this became our favorite part of our meetings.

We find that being specific with your compliments is important, such as:

**EXAMPLE**

> ✔ "Maggie, you showed kindness this week when you helped Mrs. Kiley with the groceries."
>
> ✔ "Kyle, I liked it when you included your little brother, Jimmy, when your friends were visiting."

You can use this opportunity to make a situation better. For example,

> ✔ "I think Caitlin learned something this week from her experience... "

Taking time to acknowledge the compliments is an important part of this process. Learning to receive compliments and getting reinforcement for giving them add to the value of this portion of the meeting.

# Family Discussion Topics

The topics to be discussed should be listed on an agenda, (we call ours a **Meeting Recipe Planner**) during the week leading up to your family meeting. The Leader brings up each topic, one at a time, and gives the Talking Torch to the person who wrote it on the Planner. Discussions and solutions follow. Remember, not every topic needs to be or can be solved right away. If you must, move on and follow up at your next week's meeting. Also, discussion topics do not have to be problems. They could be questions about world events, physical development, the family environment, etc.

**IDEA**

## Suggestions for Family Discussion:

✔ What did you do that you are most proud of this week?

✔ What was your biggest challenge?

✔ What was your biggest disappointment?

✔ What questions did you ask at school today?

✔ If you had to do the week over again, what would you do differently?

✔ What helped you to grow the most?

✔ What was the most fun?

✔ What are you looking forward to doing in the next week/month?

✔ What would you like to say about your accomplishments this past week?

✔ What would you like to accomplish this week?

✔ How can the family help you in accomplishing your goals?

It is important to note here that not every meeting will be smooth. Sometimes family discussion can bring about conflict. A certain amount of conflict is good in a family meeting format — as long as there is a way to bring the conflict to a successful resolution or conclusion. Everyone in the family must learn to trust one another. When trust exists, conflict with passionate debate can occur. It must be comfortable for family members to speak their minds. Encouraging debate from all will create commitment, accountability, and results!

Your table should become a safe place for all family members. It is also important for children to understand that while they have the right to their opinions and are encouraged to voice those opinions, parents are still the bottom-line decision makers. As we discussed earlier, some things are just non-negotiable.

# Creating a Family Vision Statement

Creating a Family Vision Statement may or may not be a major topic at your first family meeting. We refer to ours as our Family Vision Recipe. Your family may decide that they want some time to "settle in" to the family meeting process and will approach this topic in future (not too distant) meetings.

Also, your Family Vision Recipe may take a few meetings to work out. You are creating a statement that says who your family is, what you will live by, and what you will stand for. Your whole family should be involved in this process. It's important to note that you may go through several revisions before you select the Family Vision Recipe that works best for your family. We want our Family Vision Recipe in front of us all the time. We write it on our special tablecloth in the center. Our suggestion is to have it displayed in a prominent focal point where your family eats.

# Quick Start for Family Values Discussions at Meetings

As parents, we sometimes forget to actually talk or say what values are important to your family. We found a way to make them a part of our daily lives. During your weekly meetings, discuss a value or behavior that your family deems important, or that your family can work on during the week ahead. Encourage family members to live the value or behaviors during the upcoming week and at your next family meeting to share their success stories.

Values are fundamental principles that help us to know right from wrong and guide us in our everyday lives. It is important to talk about family values and behaviors that are central to your family. Each week, choose a value or behavior that is important for your family to learn more about and describe what it means to you as a family. (The dictionary can be a good tool for this purpose.)

Encourage each family member to practice exhibiting that value or behavior during the week ahead. Then, at your next meeting, share all the learning and success stories that happened during the week. Ask each family member two questions: How did you apply the value in your day-to-day activities, and how did the world receive it?

Our family has a 'bonus' behavior that we discuss at each meeting… laughter. We share at the table how we made someone laugh that week. It is amazing to hear the stories from all of us how we think we made a sad day for someone better, or how we think we helped spread laughter in a "pay it forward" type way.

To get started, use value and behavior ingredients from the list below and mix in some of your own.

**MEAL TIME**

# INGREDIENTS:

| | |
|---|---|
| ✔ Kindness | ✔ Understanding |
| ✔ Reverence | ✔ Patience |
| ✔ Service | ✔ Compassion |
| ✔ Justice | ✔ Courage |
| ✔ Resilience | ✔ Love |
| ✔ Responsibility | ✔ Cheerfulness |
| ✔ Friendship | ✔ Honesty |
| ✔ Generosity | ✔ Trust |
| ✔ Loyalty | ✔ Respect |
| ✔ Confidence | ✔ Fairness |
| ✔ Caring | ✔ Self-restraint |
| ✔ Humor | ✔ Forgiveness |

Remember that family meetings, with their inclusion of all members and the discussion of values, can go a long way towards revitalizing the parent-child bond and creating positive sibling relationships in today's fast-paced society. It's about improving self-esteem and learning how each person can grow to become happy, fulfilled, and productive adults. Family meetings provide a forum for making group decisions, assigning responsibilities, sharing positive feelings, and choosing and remembering fun family activities.

# Family Fun Time

Always remember that you need to keep these meetings fun (in addition to the million other things you need to think about!) One idea to make your Family Meeting special is to play a game after your meeting concludes. The Leader can choose something simple or a favorite board game could be played. This will further your bonding and add additional flavor to your time together. We have found that our children can share even more feelings during this relaxed game time.

**TOGETHER**

Now that we've discussed the nuts and bolts of how a family meeting is run, in the next chapters we'll address how to discuss particularly important issues in the family meeting setting.

# Chapter Six

# Chapter Seven
## Battling the Influence of Pop Culture

### Your Family is More Important Than MTV

> "I am not a role model. Parents should be role models."
> Charles Barkley, former NBA player and U.S. Olympian

QUOTES

Unless you're raising your kids in a cave on the side of a mountain somewhere, with no radio, TV or Internet access, your children are receiving all sorts of messages everyday. And it should go without saying that most of us don't completely agree with the messages that pop culture bombards our kids with.  But how can you fight against something that is everywhere you look?

The answer is simple, but in reality it's hard to do.  To make sure that your kids don't solely rely on role models from MTV or whatever the latest cool TV show, interactive video game, Web site, movie or clothing store catalog celebrity is, you've got to provide them with strong role models at home.  If all they see on TV, or all they hear on CD's is how much fun it is to get high, or to have sex, then it seems to follow that you can be pretty sure they're going to start engaging in that sort of behavior.

That might not be the case at all, as long as you're providing stable role models at home. You can actually show your kids that life really isn't anything at all like what they see portrayed in popular entertainment. One of the most easily attacked aspects of contemporary pop culture is how far removed it is from the reality that most Americans exist in everyday. TV and movies seem to inevitably focus on hip, rich and unattached beautiful people in New York or LA, while the vast majority of us actually live in some sort of a family setting someplace else in the great expanse of land that lay between the two big media centers. You just need to continually point out to your kids that what they see on *The Real World* is not really the real world at all.

**QUOTES**

> The theory that media messages determine people's lives and values, and the theory that media messages only mirror people's lives and values, would both require some resemblance between media messages and the lives and values of most Americans – and that resemblance does not, thank goodness, exist.
>
> **Michael Medved**, host of a
> nationally syndicated radio talk show

When Neal and I are watching TV with the kids, we always try and follow a few simple rules. First, we always try and know what they're watching. There's plenty of stuff on TV these days that isn't even appropriate for adults, let alone kids! Second, we're not afraid to turn off the TV when something inappropriate comes up during a show – and then we discuss why we turned it off. We've found that you really need to be vigilant about what sorts of popular entertainment your kids are exposed to. The new television devices such as those that pause live TV are great. You can pause the program to discuss a topic, and after the discussion you can resume the show.

# TV May be the Easiest Pop Culture to Monitor in Your Home

The new TV ratings system that you've been seeing lately has been a pretty good way to pre-judge what we'll let our kids watch. When you see these ratings in the listings or when they flash up on the screen, it's pretty hard to catch exactly what they mean, but if you take a little while to familiarize yourself with them, they can be a great help. To find a TV show's rating, you can check: 1) your local newspaper listing 2) TV Guide 3) an on-screen display at the beginning of each show or, 4) an on-screen cable program guide. Some television broadcasts and cable networks even list the program ratings on their Web sites.

Of course, you'll have to decide for yourselves at just what ages you'll let your kids see what shows on TV, and nobody will know better than you. Children mature at different rates, and the sort of thing that might confuse or upset one kid at the age of twelve might be totally acceptable to another nine year old.

Remember that sometimes exposure to age-inappropriate television shows occur when parents watch their favorite shows in the presence of their children. Whether it's an hour of *Oprah* during the day or a half-hour of a *Seinfeld* re-run in the evening, these seemingly innocent television breaks inadvertently expose our children to issues and images that they aren't ready for. As hard as it may be, we need to discipline ourselves to use the VCR and watch adult programming when our kids aren't lurking behind the couch!

**FUN FACT**

# Understanding the TV Ratings

✔ **TV-Y**

## All Children

This program is designed to be appropriate for all children. Whether animated or live-action, the themes and elements in this program are specifically designed for a very young audience, including children from ages 2 - 6. This program is not expected to frighten younger children.

✔ **TV-Y7**

## Directed to Older Children

This program is designed for children age 7 and above. It may be more appropriate for children who have acquired the developmental skills needed to distinguish between make-believe and reality. Themes and elements in this program may include mild fantasy violence or comedic violence, or may frighten children under the age of 7. Therefore, parents may wish to consider the suitability of this program for their very young children.

✔ **TV-Y7-FV**

## Directed to Older Children - Fantasy Violence

For those programs where fantasy violence may be more intense or more combative than other programs in this category, such programs will be designated TV-Y7-FV.

✔ **TV-G**

## General Audience

Most parents would find this program suitable for all ages. Although this rating does not signify a program designed specifically for children, most parents may let younger children watch this program unattended. It contains little or no violence, no strong language and little or no sexual dialogue or situations.

## ✔ TV-PG
### Parental Guidance Suggested

This program contains material that parents may find unsuitable for younger children. Many parents may want to watch it with their younger children. The theme itself may call for parental guidance and/or the program contains one or more of the following: moderate violence (V), some sexual situations (S), infrequent coarse language (L), or some suggestive dialogue (D).

## ✔ TV-MA
### Parents Strongly Cautioned

This program contains some material that many parents would find unsuitable for children less than 14 years of age. Parents are strongly urged to exercise greater care in monitoring this program and are cautioned against letting children under the age of 14 watch unattended. This program contains one or more of the following: intense violence (V), intense sexual situations (S), strong coarse language (L), or intensely suggestive dialogue (D).

The TV Parental Guidelines Monitoring Board

# If You Can Afford a Newer TV, Buy One!

Of course, you can get around all of this by buying a new TV set. It may not be economically feasible for you right now, but you could start saving some money and buy a new set with a "V" chip that will enable you to filter out anything that you feel is inappropriate. It's really a wonderful help when you're trying to monitor your kid's pop culture intake.

With a newer TV, you can actually block programs from coming into your home simply based on the rating system we discussed above. This is a great help! Even when you're not in the room with your kids, you can stop them from watching inappropriate shows or even inappropriate movies on pay cable stations. And after the kids go to bed, you can use your password on the TV and watch whatever it is you may, as a responsible adult, choose to watch.

Here's some information on V-Chips from our friends at The TV Parental Guidelines Monitoring Board:

✔ **Is there a V-Chip in every television?**
The V-Chip is in every television set 13 inches or larger manufactured after January 2000 and some sets sold after July 1, 1999. This means if you bought a new television set after July 1, 1999, your television is most likely equipped with a V-Chip.

✔ **How do I program and activate the V-Chip?**
Each television set's V-Chip works a little differently. Once you understand the definition of each rating and content label, programming and activating the V-Chip is as simple as following the set-up procedure which can be found in one of two places: 1) the television on-screen menu options, or 2) the written instruction guide included in the owner's manual. The V-Chip will only be

activated if you select the option to do so.

✔ **How do I ensure that my child will not de-activate the V-Chip?**
To activate the V-Chip, a parental lock code is required. This identification number acts as the password to activate, de-activate, and change the settings of the V-Chip.

✔ **Does the V-Chip turn off when I turn my television off?**
Turning the television off will not turn off the V-Chip. It will continue to block programs when the television is turned on again.

✔ **What type of programming does the V-Chip block?**
The V-Chip can block programming by age-based category or content label. For instance, if you want to block all TV-14 programs, you can do so by selecting TV-14. If you only want to block TV-14 programs that contain higher levels of violence, you can select TV-14-V. You should also know that when you block a particular rating or content label, all categories above that will be blocked. For example, if you block all TV-14 programs, all TV-MA programs will also be blocked. If you block TV-14-V programs, all TV-MA-V programs will also be blocked.

✔ **Can the V-Chip block out motion pictures that carry the MPAA rating?**
Motion pictures that are uncut and unedited can run on premium channels (e.g. HBO and Showtime). You can set the V-Chip to block these programs using the MPAA rating system

The TV Parental Guidelines Monitoring Board

So, there are people out there trying to help you shield your kids from negative messages on TV. Of course, you can't just rely on the ratings and the V-chips, because you may feel the ratings are either too liberal or too stringent. You really need to know what your kids are watching all the time.

# Movies and Records Have Rating Systems Too

**QUOTES**

"Since children today lack the stable family structure of past generations, they are more vulnerable to role models and authority figures outside established patriarchal institutions. I see the family as a haven of moral stability, while popular music—e.g. rock music—is a poisonous source infecting the youth of the world with messages they cannot handle."

Tipper Gore

Remember back in the 1980s, when Tipper Gore spearheaded the Parents Music Resource Center (PMRC) and tried to get the recording industry to let parents have a better idea of what was actually on the records their kids were listening to? The PMRC was composed of several wives of senators, congressmen, cabinet officials and notable businessman. It also had had support from 700 Club minister Pat Robertson and television host Sheila Walsh.

The organization was full of Moms like Susan Baker, who had overheard her 7-year-old daughter singing along to Madonna's "Like A Virgin," and was just trying to figure out how to keep her child away from songs like that until she was at least old enough to actually *understand* the messages they were sending.

Although the PMRC's goal was to "educate and inform," the group found itself fighting off accusations of promoting censorship. At times it did seem like that was what Tipper and her friends were trying to do, but Neal and I felt that their hearts were in the right place. A lot of what is played on the radio and MTV is not for kids (and to be fair, the artists really aren't writing the music for kids) and parents really should have some kind of warning system that they can rely on.

The PMRC didn't end up accomplishing much except getting record companies to put a label, which spells out in block letters "Parental Advisory: Explicit Content," on the packaging and advertising for music recordings at the discretion of individual music companies and their recording artists.

The labels help parents a little bit, but we've found that they're pretty vague. Like with TV and the ratings they put on movies, these are really only a guide and we as parents really have to monitor what our kids are seeing and hearing. And if we expand our discussion to include the FM radio stations, we just don't let the kids listen to "shock jocks" at all!

# Internet

In this day and age, there is no escaping the Internet and what our children are exposed to, either on purpose or by accident. Once my daughter mistyped "Yahoo"... and WOW! Some of the filthiest things imaginable popped right up for her to see. There are some software programs such as Net Nanny that will block some of the ruder stuff, but we as parents have to closely monitor our children activities on the Internet.

The bottom line is, even if you're being extra vigilant, you can only really monitor what sort of pop culture messages your kids receive within the walls of your own home. Once they get on the school bus, or go over to their friends' homes, all bets are off. They could be hearing and seeing anything! So, what we've found we have to do is create strong enough role models in our own home so that our kids won't have to go looking for role models among the pop culture icons of the day. And if they are away from home and see something inappropriate they will walk away from it. They become their own censors! It's not an easy thing to do, but we do have some tips that can help you get started.

**WARNING**

# How to Be a Great Role Model

**QUOTES**

> "Values don't come from a textbook or from discussions about abstract concepts. Children learn values long before they have the ability to read about them or discuss them. Rather, values are taught during the ordinary interactions of everyday life. If a child likes and respects you and your values, he will want to embrace them and make them his own."
>
> Elizabeth Berger, M.D., author of
> *Raising Children with Character*

Here's some good news: studies have actually shown that a lot of today's kids do see their parents as role models. An online survey, conducted by Harris Interactive, focused on more than 370 girls aged 12 through 18. The results show that girls and young women take a strong stand when it comes to the ideals that are truly long-lasting. And mothers and friends scored high as sources of trusted advice; 46 percent of respondents chose their moms and 40 percent chose their friends; only 4 percent said that they thought a celebrity like Drew Barrymore would provide good advice.

So, at least we've got 46% of our kid's attention! And there was more good news: when the survey asked young women to rate the power of fashion magazines, 55% said that magazines "promote unrealistic images" of women, while only four percent said that magazines "play the right role" in portraying women.

All this survey offers is a little hope that kids can still respond to parents as role models, despite being bombarded with pop culture every time they stick their head out the front door. But it does reinforce that we as parents need to be mindful of that fact, and need to strive to be better role models every day.

# Do as I Say and Not as I Do

It should go without saying that if we want our kids to behave in certain ways, then we have to exhibit those behaviors ourselves. We need to strive to be living, day-to-day examples of our family's own personal value systems. Everyday, in as many situations as we can, we need to show the compassion, honesty, generosity and openness we want our children to have.

We need to examine our own behavior. If we abuse drugs or alcohol, or if we're dishonest in our everyday dealings, our kids are going to pick up on it. If you're engaging in little, seemingly harmless activities like ignoring traffic laws, being discourteous to strangers, or if you laugh at a drunk or stoned person in a movie, you may be sending the wrong message to your child. The list is literally endless! But if we strive to watch ourselves a little more everyday, and work just a little bit on being the person we really want to be, we'll find that we can really exhibit the qualities that we want our kids to pick up from us.

You don't need to change everything you're doing overnight. Just by the fact that you're taking the time to read this book, it shows that you're a caring parent who is making an effort to make the world a better place for your kids. So, you're probably well on your way to being a good role model – to being the kind of person that you want your kids to be.

**REMEMBER**

Here's a tip sheet from the National PTA that Neal and I found useful, a sort of primer on what it takes to be a good parental role model. While its focus was on drug usage, we adapted it a bit so that you can pretty much take the advice and apply it to all behaviors that we would like our kids to emulate.

**IDEA**

## Tip sheet: 10 Ways to Be a Great Role Model

Remember -- you are your children's most important example. They learn by observing you, even when you don' know it. If this sounds a bit daunting, don't worry. Here are 10 ways to be a great role model, and chances are you're already doing many of them.

**1. Share your values with your children.**
Don't assume your children know your family's values – talk about these topics often. Offer guidance to teach your children other important values such as being honest, reliable and responsible.

**2. Demonstrate your own sense of self-respect and self-esteem.**
Take good care of yourself by following a healthful diet, exercising regularly and making time for relaxation. You'll provide valuable behaviors for your children to imitate (and you'll feel better, too!).

**3. Show that you value your independence.**
Let your children know – by your words and your actions – that you don't have to "follow the crowd" but prefer to make your own decisions.

**4. Set a good example when using medications.**
Be cautious about how you use prescription drugs and even over-the-counter medicines. Show that you can deal with mild pain or tension without turning to medications. Instruct your child never to take any medication without your permission.

**5. If you drink alcohol, demonstrate responsibility.**
Use alcohol in moderation and avoid using excuses for drinking, like having a rough day. How you use alcohol will influence your children and they will tend to have the same drinking habits you do when they grow up. Never allow children to mix drinks or serve them to guests, and never serve alcohol to children, not even beer or wine.

**6. Set a good example for dealing with stress.**
If you have stress or conflict in your life, talk about it honestly with your children. They need to know that such struggles are a natural and normal part of life. It's how you deal with these struggles that are important.

**7. Share your successes – and failures – with your children.**
Perhaps you're trying to lose weight, quit smoking or adopt a healthier lifestyle. When you're making an effort to change your own behavior, talk about it openly with your children. It's OK to let them know when you've failed or fallen short of a goal – and it may make it easier for them to tell you when they've made a mistake. You're also conveying an important message that change isn't easy and mistakes are opportunities for learning.

**8. Show that you love and value each member of your family.**
Let your children know that spending time together is something you look forward to. Make plans ahead of time to do special things such as going to a movie or museum. Also enjoy spur-of-the-moment activities – going out for ice cream or taking a walk after a rainstorm.

**9. Discuss how the media portray alcohol, tobacco and drugs.**
Talk with your children about images and messages conveyed by television, music, movies billboards and other media that glamorize alcohol and other drugs. Let them know what you think and guide them in recognizing the other side of what appears to be glamorous.

**10. Take a genuine interest in your children's school and your community.**
Support school and community programs that benefit children. Give your time as a volunteer. Attend functions to show your children you're interested in their activities. When your time is limited, make an effort to keep in touch with other parents to share ideas about how adults can set good examples for our children.

> adapted from COMMON SENSE: Strategies for Raising
> Alcohol- and Drug-free Children, The National PTA

# How to Find the Good Stuff in Pop Culture

**TOGETHER**

The last thing I want to do is to sound like Chicken Little, and run around squawking that all pop culture is evil, and that if we let our kids buy a CD, watch some TV or play certain video games they're all going to end up in Satanic cults. While a lot of pop culture is pure garbage, there are definitely some good lessons to be learned in pop culture too. Believe it or not, there are some entertainers who actively strive to send positive and life-affirming messages in their art. The trick is in ferreting out those messages.

We put our heads together with the Dunns and came up with some exercises that you can do with your family during your weekly family meetings. These exercises will help your kids learn how to extract the good messages in popular culture while strengthening their resistance to the negative messages.

You should try doing these exercise once every few months – if you do them too infrequently, the kids will forget what they've learned, so bear in mind that these exercises do need to be repeated. At that same time, if you do this every week, the kids will get bored with it and just start to tune them out. Nobody knows your kids' attention spans better than you do, so you'll need to figure out when to work them into your family meeting schedule.

# Exercises for Battling the Influence of Pop Culture

**Step 1:** Get a cardboard box, and write in big letters on the side "Pop Culture Bin." Put it somewhere in the house that everybody can get to.

Do this at the end of your family meeting the week before you want to try these exercises.

**IDEA**

> **Big Hint #1:** By calling it a bin, you'll be sending a subtle subconscious message to your kids that most of pop culture is disposable!

**Step 2:** Throughout the week, have each family member gather various items related to their favorite pop culture idols. These could be musicians, actors, TV characters, politicians, TV evangelists, cartoon or video characters, comic book heroes or villains… anyone or anything who falls into the realm of popular culture. Magazine clippings, CDs, and videos are just a few examples of things to put into the box.

**Step 3:** At the meeting, each family member takes a turn and shares some of the sights and sounds of their cultural favorites. Don't immediately fly off the handle if your kid starts playing some horribly raucous music! This exercise will create an important opportunity to understand and possibly even *appreciate* the celebrities, music, or trends that are appealing to each family member.

**WARNING**

> **Big Hint #2:** For example, it just wouldn't be productive for you to say, "How can you listen to that garbage?!" Try and remember what your parents used to say about the crazy music you listened to when you were a kid! That sort of immediate negative reaction is what we're trying to overcome here! The focus of this exercise is to try and create an opportunity to *connect*, not to immediately criticize. If criticism is called for, that comes later in the discussion.

**Step 4:** After the kids present what they feel is *positive* about the cultural favorites they shared; the family can then discuss the potentially

**TOGETHER**

*negative* impact of these cultural influences.  As part of this process, the family can:

✔ Listen to song lyrics and talk about how they reflect or clash with your personal family values.

✔ Look at magazine and catalog images and explore how realistic or unrealistic they may be and how they make each family member feel about themselves (this is also a wonderful chance to discuss the reality that most pictures of pop culture icons are airbrushed, unrealistic, and the body shapes they represent are unhealthy to maintain!).  Ask your kids if they know any "real" people who look like that?

✔ Parents can share some of the sights and sounds of the "oldies" and share their observations of how culture has changed since they were children.  You might be surprised to realize how much your favorites have in common with your kid's favorites!

# What Have We Learned?

After reading this chapter, you should have a heightened awareness that there are some organizations out there that are trying to make it easier for you to monitor your children's pop culture intake.  You should also be thinking everyday about how, with just a little effort, you can mold yourself into a better role model for your kids.

And maybe the biggest takeaway from this chapter is that you can feel good about the fact that if you actually do the exercises you just read about you'll have an easily accomplished, simple and structured way to talk to your kids about the positive and negative influences that can be found in pop culture.  Who knows?  You just might find out that you're a bigger fan of hip-hop than you ever thought you were!

# Chapter Eight
## Family Issues and Roles

## Importance of Roles

> Roles play an extremely important part in healthy family functioning. Most researchers agree that the establishment of clear roles within a family is directly connected to a family's ability to deal with day-to-day life, unforeseen crises, and the normal changes that occur in families over time. Family roles are patterns of behavior by which individuals fulfill family functions and needs.
>
>     Rick Peterson, Assistant Professor,
>     Department of Human Development, Virginia Tech

**QUOTES**

One important thing to understand about your family, as you sit down to your family meals and meetings, is just what your family thinks about itself. Do you think your family life is strong? Is that feeling echoed or argued by other family members? Is everybody in the family perceived as "pulling their weight" or doing whatever it takes to contribute their part?

A recent national survey showed that strong families have six common strengths. Do you see these as strengths or weaknesses in your family? The survey showed that strong families:

✔ **Show appreciation for each other.**
   They compliment each other to make other family members feel appreciated and good about themselves.

✔ **Deal with crisis in a positive manner.**
They serve as a great strength to each other during times
of adversity.

✔ **Spend time together.**
They structure their schedules so they can be together more often.

✔ **Have a strong commitment to their families.**
They invest time and energy in each other because family is their
number one priority.

✔ **Have good communication patterns.**
They talk with each other, and, more importantly, they listen to
each other, as well.

✔ **Have a high degree of spiritual orientation.**
A spiritual lifestyle tends to make them more forgiving, respectful,
patient, and positive.

Figuring out just how your family views itself may go a long way
towards helping you to structure your family meals and meetings.
When Neal and I began to really talk to our kids about what our
family's strengths are, we were pleasantly surprised by some of what
we heard, and we also realized there were areas that we needed to
work on.

One of the things I've discovered through my research is that clear,
flexible roles are one of the keys to a successful family life. Families who
understand where everybody fits into the overall picture seem to be
able to deal with everyday family life more easily, and are better
equipped to handle unexpected family crises. In families where clear,
flexible roles exist, individual members will be much more likely to take
their responsibilities seriously.

# How Do Members See Themselves in the Family Structure?

We, as young children, decide how to live. The whiny, sickly child gets attention; the mean, strong-willed, rebellious kid gets his way; the conforming, quiet child is appreciated; the good kid is loved. We learn to expect to be winners or losers. These are all preschool choices… and they influence us for an entire lifetime.

Dr. Clay Tucker-Ladd, in Psychological Self-Help

**QUOTES**

Everybody figures out where they fit in the family structure pretty early on in their lives, whether they realize it or not. It's usually not a conscious decision, just something that people fall into. Everybody needs to know what niche they fill in the family. Research indicates that if you can nudge yourself and your family into healthy roles, your children will have a better chance of growing up into well-adjusted and mentally healthy adults.

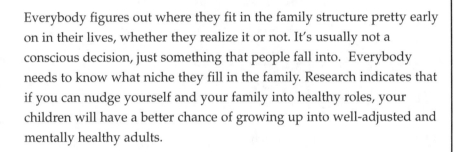

**Do not fall into the trap of pigeonholing children into the funny one, smart one, cute one, etc. That is NOT what the idea of clear roles is really about. There can be two funny ones, two leaders, etc. in any family.**

**WARNING**

Your family has to make many everyday decisions about who will be responsible for completing a certain task and chores or who will take on a particular responsibility. For example, families must decide who will take out the trash, who will mow the lawn, who will walk the dog – and who will clean up the dog poop! – who takes the kids to school, who will cook dinner on what nights, who does the dishes, who will watch the children after they return from school, and who will work

**119**

and provide financial support for the family… the list goes on and on!

In healthy families, roles are spread out so that no one family member ever feels like they are taking on too much of the burden of everyday life. We try and make sure that each one of our kids knows exactly what is expected of them on a daily basis. Some roles, such as childcare, are important family tasks that should be shared if at all possible.

Roles and responsibilities go far beyond everyday chores like feeding the goldfish. Your kids should know that they are responsible for each other. If one of your kids sees that their brother or sister is having a hard time with something, or is about to make an unwise choice, they should know that they need to step up and help their sibling.

# Four Roles Essential in a Strong Family

**IDEA**

I've found, through my research, that you can break down just what roles a family needs to fulfill before you can think of yourself as a healthy family. Now, within these big four roles are the niches you and your kids will fill in – the big four just give you an overall idea of what ground you need to cover.

✔ **Providing Resources**
This is absolutely the most basic role of a family. Simply put, providing resources like food, clothing, and shelter, for all family members is the first step.

✔ **Love and Affection**
Just like the first role, this is so basic that it is almost taken for granted. Family members need to provide the love and affection that develops into an atmosphere of comfort, warmth, and reassurance for all family members. This ranges from a simple kiss

at the breakfast table to a parent or sibling comforting a child after he/she has a bad day at school, or a bad experience in a little league game, to family members holding one another and supporting each other after the death of a loved one.

✔ **Teach Your Children Well**
From the Bible to Crosby, Stills and Nash, people have been telling you all along to teach your children well. And it's true: when you have children you have a sacred trust to help with the physical, emotional, educational, and social development of your kids. Examples of this role are a parent helping a child make it through school, older brothers and sister helping their younger sibs learn how to deal with things, or a parent helping a young adult son or daughter decide on a career path.

✔ **Maintaining and Managing the Whole Journey!**
This fourth part covers a lot of ground and includes family leadership, decision-making, handling family finances, and maintaining appropriate roles with respect to extended family, friends, neighbors and society at large. This also includes making rules for the family, maintaining discipline and making sure that you and your kids are living up to the behavioral standards you've set.

When you look at it like that, the idea of the things your family needs to do seem both simple and complex at the same time, don't they? That's because the roles are so obvious you never really think of them, but when you actually look at them in black and white on a piece of paper you begin to realize the enormity of it all. Relax. You're probably already taking care of all these things, you just never took the time to sit down and figure out how you're actually doing it. And after reading this chapter and examining just how your family functions, and who is carrying the load in what roles, you'll be able to figure out how to do all this stuff on a more even and efficient basis.

# Suggestions for Developing Healthy Family Roles

**QUOTES**

> Psychologists say that significant stressors for some adults and kids are role confusion ("I don't know what I'm responsible for") and "role strain." Awareness of and discussion about these ideas are more common in the workplace, but they apply equally to families like yours... Role strain happens when an adult or child is unclear on (confused about) or uninterested in their group responsibilities, and/or... feels inadequate to do them competently, and/or... they have concurrent roles that conflict and/or are collectively overwhelming.
>
> Peter Gerlach, MSW, in *About Family Roles and Role Conflicts: Help each other agree on who's responsible for what*

But how do you assign family roles? Keeping in mind how each family member feels about the state of your family might be helpful when you're sorting this out. The assigning and carrying out of family roles can be a difficult task, especially when you may be battling against pre-conceived perceptions about how your family works and what roles each member plays in it.

This may seem like a tremendous amount of effort to go through; I'm basically asking you to examine something that may seem to be working pretty well already. But I can't stress enough how important it is for individual family members to know where they fit into the family.

## Establish Clear Roles

Listed below are some tips that we've adapted from the work of Rick Peterson and Stephen Green of the Department of Human Development at Virginia Tech that can help make this process easier for your family:

✔ Roles should be clearly identifiable. Individual family members must know and acknowledge their roles and responsibilities. For example, in healthy families, mothers and fathers have a clear understanding of their role as parents. They are to provide physical resources (e.g., food, clothing, and shelter), discipline, and a supportive, nurturing environment that facilitates their children's physical and emotional development.

✔ Children should have clearly defined roles and responsibilities also. Regular chores should be assigned on a daily or weekly basis. And children should know that there are rewards or consequences associated with doing or not doing those chores.

✔ Families that are having difficulties often find that their family roles are not well defined and individual members do not understand what is expected of them. Establishing clear roles helps a family function more effectively because each member knows what he/she is expected to accomplish, and there is a clear idea of what he/she can count on other family members to do. If these individuals fail to fulfill their roles then other family members might have to do extra work, making them feel resentful and overburdened, thus hurting the functioning of the family.

**REMEMBER**

## Allow for Flexibility

✔ Flexibility in roles is essential in a healthy family. Family roles
naturally change over time. They also may change during times of
crisis, such as when a family member becomes seriously ill or
unexpectedly dies. The difference between healthy and unhealthy
families in these situations is the healthy family's ability to adjust
and adapt, which often requires a temporary or permanent shift in
roles. In the case of illness or death, it is sometimes necessary for
other family members to take on additional roles (e.g., becoming
a financial provider). Flexibility in roles is essential in a
healthy family.

## Allocate Roles Fairly

✔ In healthy families, every member is responsible for fulfilling
certain roles. These roles are spread among the various members so
that no one is asked to take on too many responsibilities. Problems
arise if one family member is forced to fulfill too many roles. An
example of this is when fulltime working mothers are expected to
take care of the children and complete the majority of household
tasks with little assistance from other family members. It is
important to discuss, as a family, each member's understanding of
the roles he or she has been assigned. If someone feels
overburdened and unable to fulfill that particular role, then
changes may be needed. In healthy families, children are required
to take on appropriate roles of responsibility within the family.

## Be Responsible in Fulfilling Family Roles

✔ Families that function well have members who take their roles
seriously and do their best to fulfill their duties. Members who fail
to take their roles seriously, or who refuse to carry out their roles,
can create significant problems for the entire family. An example of

failing to fulfill a role is when a parent does not provide adequate physical and emotional support for his/her children. There are many problems that can result from this failure, including behavior problems, depression, and low self-esteem. When parents neglect their roles, they inadvertently may send the message that their children are not important and they model that responsibilities are to be filled when we feel like filling them. Consistently taking responsibility for one's roles contributes to a healthy family.

Now that you more fully understand the four basic roles that your family needs to fulfill, and you've got the guidelines on how to assign parts of each to individual family members, think about how your family is meeting these needs. Are you on track? Or do you need to re-examine how things get done in your family?

# Family of Origin

One way to help our children understand their role in the family is to help them place themselves in the overall family history. Often, with all the modern stresses on families, and with the way that people move around today, kids can lose sight of the fact that they are part of an overall extended family. We can work together with our kids to make sure that they don't lose sight of the fact that not only are they part of an extended family, but that they actually have some family history.

Knowing the family history on both sides of the family is important, if that's possible. Mommy and Daddy should talk with one another about their own families while growing up. How alike were they? How different? What are your family traditions, on both sides? How did they communicate with one another? It is important to understand where your spouse comes from in order to have a solid relationship in the future. Also, knowing about what made up their particular family can help your child choose the kind of person they want to partner with when it's time for them to start *their* family.

Asking Grandpa to tell the story of how the family crossed the country on a wagon train or having Grandma tell the story of how our ancestors fled Russia during the Holocaust are the kind of experiences that make history personal. Sharing stories about what kind of boy Daddy was and the funny things he did, or how Grandma met Grandpa, or how Mommy fell in love with Daddy put our relatives in social context so we can understand more about them.

Telling the stories is as therapeutic and valuable as hearing them. When our children can retell the family stories they claim a bit of the family history and our departed relatives continue to be a part of our lives. Children also love to hear stories about their younger years. Knowing how they fit into our lives as babies, how important they were, what cute things they did, etc., makes them feel good about themselves and good about their relationships in the family, past and present.

Now, it's totally up to you how far into this that you want to go. You can tell stories or draw a simple family tree, or you can dive totally into the whole deal and come up with a complete family history. But remember, people can spend years and years tracking down information on their ancestors. I'm just offering this up as a suggestion of something that might be fun and informative for you to do with older kids.

# Family Roles and Issues Exercises

## Out of the Box

**Step 1:** Get a cardboard box, and write Family Roles and Issues on the side of it. Put it somewhere in the house that everybody can get to. Do this at the end of your family meeting the week before you want to try these exercises.

**IDEA**

**Step 2:** Throughout the week the family can decorate a shoebox with family photos, magazine clippings, paint, crayons, etc. Get creative. Let the kids stick whatever they want to it.

**Step 3:** This is for the parents. Inside the box place index cards or post it notes with the following incomplete sentences:

- What I like best about our family is...

- What I most want to improve about our family is...

- The silliest person in our family is...

- The person most likely to take charge in our family is...

- Our family's best times usually involve...

- Our family's worst times usually involve...

- I am so grateful that our family...

- I hope that our family will...

- My biggest worry about our family is...

- Other family members think that I am...

- I hope our family knows that I...

**REMEMBER**

> **Big Hint #1:** The incomplete sentences that the parents put in the box will guide the family discussion. You can modify the sentences to better fit your family, or to steer the discussion in directions that you feel your family needs to explore. Don't hesitate to invite your children to contribute some incomplete sentences of their own.

**Step 4:** At your next family meeting, each family member takes turns reaching into the box and pulling out a card. They read the card and complete the sentence. The family can then respond to what is said. Next, the individual who selected the card chooses the next family member to select a card from the box.

**WARNING**

> **Big Hint #2:** Remember not to get upset if your kids come up with some pretty wacky or unexpected answers in this exercise. The whole idea is to get the kids talking about how they truly perceive your family and their place in it. There are no wrong answers here – although there may be some misconceptions or misunderstandings that you can correct in a clear and rational manner during the discussion.

**Step 5:** This procedure is continued until all family members have had a chance to complete a sentence and/or all of the cards have been removed from the box. For a longer version of the game, each card can be passed around the table so that each family member completes each card in the shoebox.

## Role Colors

**Step1:** Gather together some construction paper in a variety of colors and cut them into small strips.

**Step 2:** On the small pieces of paper write out all of the responsibilities of running your household. Brainstorm together to include as many things as you can think of, ranging from feeding the dog to bringing in the mail.

**Step 3:** Color code the paper to represent different types of responsibilities. For example, preparing breakfast, cooking dinner, setting the table, buying groceries, and unloading the dishwasher could all go on orange pieces of paper to represent the category of kitchen responsibilities. Mowing the lawn, shoveling snow off of the driveway and other outdoor activities can go on a different color paper.

> **Big Hint #1: Generating a list of the many responsibilities will amaze the whole family since we often don't realize how much each of us does to keep the household running smoothly.**

**TOGETHER**

**Step 4:** Sort the papers so that the person who is most likely to take care of that responsibility has that paper in front of them. If the responsibility or chore is shared by two or more people, just make other copies of that paper so that each person gets one.

**Step 5:** Look around the table to see the relative size of the piles in front of you. Are they even? Did you realize or appreciate how much each family member was doing? Did you not realize that you weren't doing as much as you thought you were? Remember, not all papers are equivalent in size – some responsibilities take more time and effort than others. The piles don't have to be even, they just have to be perceived as fair and equitable. It can be fun to end the exercise by offering the opportunity to trade responsibilities. Taking turns doing each other's chores can not only help you to avoid getting into a rut, but it will clearly show family members just how many roles and responsibilities there are to fill in everyday life!

# What Have We Learned?

After reading this chapter, you should better understand how your family functions, and the roles and responsibilities of each family member. You should be able to spot the strengths and weakness in your family structure, and be thinking about ways that you can use the strengths to build up those areas that may need help.

You should also feel good about the fact that if you actually do the exercises you just read about you'll have an easily accomplished, simple and structured way to talk to your kids about the family roles and issues that we discussed in this chapter. Who knows? You just might find out that your family is chugging along just like it's supposed to be, or that with a little more effort you can get right back on track.

# Chapter Nine
## School Issues

## School of Hard Knocks

I can still remember the way I felt when I walked Caitlin, our oldest, to her first day of kindergarten, I felt like I was sending my baby out onto the world all alone. What a tough day for me! Not so tough for her, though… we had prepared her well. She kissed me goodbye and ran off! I was the one who was a basket case!

When I was getting ready to send our youngest, Jimmy five years later, to his first day of kindergarten, I thought about some things that helped me get through the first days for the other kids with a little less stress:

---

### Tips for Parents Suffering the First Day of School Blues

✔ Trust that your children have the skills they need to be all right on their own.

✔ Don't forget that you've spent the last few years teaching your kids to cope with things for themselves, so you can assume they will be fine.

✔ You should feel proud that your children can be independent, for short periods of time.

✔ Think about how those first days of school were for you. Even if you had a rocky time, you survived! Your kids will too!

**REMEMBER**

131

> ✔ **Most schools in America have well-trained, competent, and caring adults to help your kids cope with these sorts of situations... they do it everyday.**
>
> ✔ **Think: you are not losing a child, you are gaining playmates!**

Of course, after I got through my emotional experience, I had to deal with the reality that my babies were going off to school and I would have to start dealing with all of the typical school issues. Things like, the work is too hard, or the work is too easy, some big kids are bothering me... the list goes on and on! So I keep myself informed on what's going on in the kids' schools as much as I can, and I rely on our family meals and meeting to keep on sending the messages the kids need to hear so that they can cope with all of the new things they're learning everyday.

# Tips on How to Get Kids Ready for the First Day of School

**FUN FACT**

> Research into early childhood development has revealed that the brain begins to develop much sooner than was earlier believed, and that without sufficient mental stimulation children may fail to develop the synapses that facilitate learning throughout their lives.
>
> National PTA

Most of you are probably already doing this, but you really need to start getting your kids ready for school years before they actually start. The best part about this is it doesn't have to cost you anything but time. Coming to the meal table as a family and having conversations is a great start. Research shows that children who regularly engage in family meals have better vocabulary and confidence than children who do not.

Get yourself a library card! You can choose from lots of great ABC books, counting books, and concept books like those by Tana Hoban to reinforce the basic skills your kids will be taught in school. Read each book at least three or four times before taking it back to the library.

Something that's really fun to do with the kids, and really a good way to jumpstart those incredible little brains is to find wordless stories like the John Goodall books and Mercer Mayer 'Frog' stories and let your child make up their own stories. This is guaranteed to be fun, and I guarantee you'll be pleasantly surprised when you see the values and ideas you're trying to pass along in your family meals and meetings cropping up in the stories they make up. And if those values and ideas *don't* start cropping up, then this is a perfect time to reinforce what you've been taking about!

**TOGETHER**

Here are some other quick tips on how to get your wee ones ready for school ahead of time:

✔ Kindergarteners need basic physical dexterity, and you should work with them so they are able to tie their shoes and hang a jacket on a hook.

✔ At the most basic level, your kids should be able to count and identify shapes by the time they enter kindergarten.

✔ Talk to children about what they think school will be like.

✔ Take care of paperwork, such as medical forms and other official documents.

✔ Sometime over the summer, take your child to visit the school building.

✔ Try to arrange a play date with future classmates.

✔ Meet with the school's principal and teachers before the school year begins.

✔ Bring your child to play on the school playground during the summer.

✔ Make sure you know if there is a dress code.

✔ Take your kids back-to-school shopping. Let them help choose school supplies, lunch boxes and new clothes.

✔ Even though I normally advocate open communication, don't let your kids know about your fears and anxieties about them starting school. They have enough on their plate already!

✔ Try and walk your kids to their classrooms on the first day of school but remember, don't stay too long! That would just make it harder on both of you!

✔ Inform the teacher if your child has allergies.

✔ Make sure they know that they need to listen to the teachers, bus drivers and aides!

✔ There are wonderful books on going to school. Audrey Penn's *The Kissing Hand*, for example, is a beautiful tale about a raccoon's fist time at school and includes a wonderful ritual (a kiss on the palm of the hand for your child to place on their cheek anytime in the day to feel your love).

Just over the last few years we've seen a frightening rise in kidnappings. I don't know if there's always been that many and because we have 24 hour-a-day news on cable now we hear more about it, but the occurrence of people snatching kids does seem to be rising. It's so important to have your child always be aware of his or her surroundings inside and outside of school. Make sure your children know to tell a teacher, or some school official, and you when they see a stranger hanging around near the school. If they catch the school bus to and from school, or walk, make sure that you either wait or walk with them, or at the very least they're walking or waiting with a group of kids. These horrible people who prey on kids almost always go after kids who are alone, so impress upon your kids that there is safety in numbers! It is also important to NOT make the kids terrified of the outside world. We need to remember that we are the parents and if someone is to be afraid it should be us. Let them be kids, *cautious and aware*, but still kids.

**WARNING**

# School is Too Hard

Most children have one thing in common -- they hate homework. Many of them complain about it being "too hard." The truth is that kids do seem to get a lot of homework these days. When you kids complain, it may be that your child is too tired or it may really be that the work is overwhelming. Now, it should go without saying that you shouldn't actually be doing your child's homework but you'll find out that occasionally it is necessary to help.

You can also help by breaking the work down into reasonable chunks. When your second grader is freaking out when she sees the sheer amount of questions she needs to answer, you can help her start by saying, "First, let's read the directions." If there is a whole sheet of twenty or so questions to answer, suggest that she do five, and then take a break together. Sometimes you can share a healthy snack when they finish a set of questions, or when they move from one subject to another.

But if your kids' homework brings on the waterworks and the weeping and wailing every night, you need to find out why. Ask the teacher if your child is the only one in the class having trouble. Ask your child if he dislikes this particular teacher. If he does, ask what makes him dislike this teacher so much? Maybe it's just a temporary problem because your child is having difficulty with new concepts presented in class that week, or it could be a sign that your child needs more help.

Teachers can definitely help with troubleshooting, and most teachers are only too glad to help. I've found that truly bad teachers are the exception, that most of the teachers my children have had are really willing to go the extra mile. Together, the teacher and you can get your child to thrive in school.

If your child is having real academic difficulty, many schools are willing to devise an individual educational plan. There are all sorts of alternatives: certain homework assignments may be scaled down, your child may be given longer deadlines, or may be allowed to do alternative assignments suited to her learning style. Some kids are hands-on learners who might be able to build a paddleboat instead of writing a science paper. Obviously, a lot of this depends on the school and the teacher and how involved and assertive you choose to be when it comes to your child's education.

Your kids need to know that they have options and help available to them. This is a perfect situation for them to practice the assertive communication skills we discussed in Chapter Six.

Here are some tips to pass onto your kids when schoolwork becomes too hard for them:

**IDEA**

✔ Be honest and admit what you do not know.

✔ Take time to talk with the teacher outside of class.

✔ Ask for help or a tutor.

✔ Have your mom, dad, and you meet with the teacher to see how you can catch up on your work.

✔ Just relax. Take a deep breath and take one step at a time.

✔ Write a letter to your teacher and explain how you feel.

✔ Be willing to work extra hard to catch up on your work.

✔ Always ask your teacher to explain things again or in a different way.

✔ Look for computer programs to help you learn.

✔ Others will be willing to help you learn.

✔ If you do your best, no one can blame you.

✔ Never give up; ask questions over and over.

✔ Focus on all that you do know, as you are working to catch up on your work.

> Randolph Elementary School, Kid to Kid
> Information for Elementary Military School Students

In some cases, homework anxiety is a byproduct of a teacher's high expectations. If you are concerned that your child's teacher may have developmentally inappropriate expectations, schedule a meeting with the teacher to learn more about what she/he expects from the students. Use your good communication skills to learn more about the teacher's thoughts about what is appropriate and share what has been going on at home when homework is attempted. Ask for some suggestions to help your child be more successful in completing assignments.

In the event that communication with the teacher is unsuccessful – if you don't feel your concerns are being taken seriously, you can't work together toward solutions, or you conclude that the teacher is being unfair or unreasonable in some way – then it may be necessary to consult with the school principal. Ask other parents how their children are doing and if there is consensus that the teacher is putting undue pressure on the students, work together to see that change takes place.

Parents shouldn't teach their children that when they have a hard time reaching high expectations it is appropriate to attack the teacher... or someday the boss. All too often we see students who have learned that the goal is to get out of any assignment that seems too tough, assuming that the assignment is unfair rather than taking the responsibility to work harder. Having high expectations is not necessarily a bad thing!

One other point: sometimes your kid just may be resistant to working on homework with you because they feel added pressure not to let their parents down. Maybe you need to back off a little bit. Try to find someone other than yourself to help your child with homework. You may need to hire a tutor; sometimes the babysitter or the high school kid next door can help your third grader master the multiplication tables. It's worth a shot!

# School is Too Easy

Teenagers nationwide have issued a decisive verdict on their high schools. A new study reports that most think their classes are not challenging enough, often lack exemplary teachers and are filled with too many disruptive students. The study, conducted by the national non-profit group Public Agenda, sketches a portrait of American high schools in which most students are coasting through their classes – and know it.

Public Agenda

**FUN FACT**

Having our children sail through school with little effort sounds like a problem that most of us would like to have, but believe me, this can be just as hard to deal with as when your child is having a tough time with the schoolwork. Kids who find their schoolwork too easy can sometimes become bored in class, act out and disrupt the learning experience for everyone else.

Neal and I have a friend who is now a professional writer that had this problem when he was in school. In elementary school, he had teachers who realized he was exceptionally bright and he was in a school where they had classes for gifted children – they studied the Greek classics *The Iliad* and *The Odyssey* in the fifth grade! But by middle school, when he was in a building with a few thousand other kids, he was no longer getting the special attention he received in elementary school.

Bored with schoolwork, he became a behavior problem, and started to hang around with other kids that were acting out in class, or cutting classes. Since he was so bright he could drop into class from time to time and catch up with the other kids, and do just well enough on the tests so that he would squeak by. He graduated, but never really had a high school education at all!

He then proceeded to work a series of dead end jobs for the next few years. He never even considered college because he had never really learned a thing in high school! He ended up a desperately unhappy young man, drinking too much – it wasn't until he wrapped his car around a tree one night that he realized that he was out of control, and that he had to change his way of life. But the root of his problem, and what caused all his troubles later on, was simply that his schoolwork was too easy and he got bored. So, even though the story has a happy ending for our friend, you can see how it can be a major problem when school is too easy.

# So What Should We Do if School is Too Easy?

The things parents need to do when school is too easy are not that different than what you need to do when school is too hard. You need to talk to your child's teacher. Make an appointment to sit down with the teacher to discuss the work your kid is doing. During your meeting, share your observations of your child's reading and academic skills and describe the ways in which you would like to see your child challenged at school. Brainstorm some ideas that will facilitate your child's educational growth.

You already know that a child's education is the result of the partnership between teachers and parents so don't worry about being too pushy. As long as you remain positive and constructive during all your discussions, your child's teacher will most likely appreciate your support, advice, and involvement. Nobody likes to feel attacked, so be sure that what you have to say is specifically focused on how your child can get the most out of school (e.g., avoid saying things like "You are too easy" or "You aren't giving our child enough to do.") And just like we said when school was too hard, if you don't make headway with the teacher, then you need to talk to the principal. If it seems that the pace and level of work are right on target for the other students in class, you may have an academically talented child who would benefit from a gifted program or honors classes. Ask the school guidance counselor how to have your child tested and considered for placement in a more challenging environment.

Finally, make sure that you congratulate your children on doing so well in school. Give them praise often, and continue to make good reading materials available at home.

Once again, your kids also need to know that they have options and help available to them. This is yet another perfect situation for them to practice the assertive communication skills we discussed in Chapter Six.

Here are some tips to pass onto your kids when schoolwork becomes too easy for them:

**IDEA**

✔ Set time to visit with your teacher. Explain that the work is too easy for you. Save examples to show you can already do what the class is doing. Ask if your work can be more challenging.

✔ Be polite and visit with your teacher at time where no one else is there.

✔ Write a letter to your teacher to explain how you feel about repeating work you have already done and learned.

✔ Visit with the counselor or principal.

✔ Set up a conference with mom, dad and the new teacher to explain concerns.

✔ See if there are others like you in the class who feel work is easy. Work with them on similar interests with the teacher's permission.

✔ Write a story about a child who is like you and can do work beyond what others are doing. Include a solution.

✔ See if there is a gifted program at school.

Randolph Elementary School, Kid to Kid Information for Elementary Military School Students

Remember, this can be just as much of a problem as when your child is struggling to keep up. Ask your kids how they feel about their schoolwork, and take the appropriate actions. Who knows, maybe you'll get lucky, and school will proceed at exactly the right pace for your kids!

# My Kid is Being Bullied at School

QUOTES

"Bullying has been defined as "the tendency for some children to frequently oppress, harass or intimidate other children, verbally, physically or both, in and out of school." It is not the minor behavior problems that are a part of growing up, such as horseplay, occasional good-natured teasing or even the odd physical scrap between children of equal strength.
Richard B. Goldbloom, M.D

The only good news about bullies and bullying is that schools are finally waking up to the fact that they need to do something about it. We've all heard enough of the isolated horror stories about how bullied kids end up committing suicide or bringing in weapons to school to take their revenge in a horrible public display of retribution. Now schools are finally taking this major problem seriously, and they're getting proactive in their attempts to stamp out this dangerous anti-social behavior.

> Bullies and schools have been a function of one another since classrooms first appeared. Over time, either being a bully or being bullied has become a part of the lore of school and a rite of passage that most kids experience at some point.
> Kathleen Sheridan, Metropolitan Family Services' Teased and Bullied Program

**QUOTES**

Researchers have found that up to 15% of school children admit they have been bullied, and that part of the difficulty in dealing with bullying has been that victims often are reluctant to say anything about it. Bullies use intimidation to hurt and silence the children they pick out to prey upon. In days gone by, like when we were all in school, the tactics bullies use to create fear and humiliation may have seemed, to adults, like harmless childhood nonsense. We know better now – we know that bullying leaves scars upon the victims and can also escalate to almost unbelievable levels.

So how can you tell if your child is being bullied? Most kids won't tell you, because an essential part of bullying is the threat of reprisals if the victims "tell." But certain symptoms should make you suspicious. Look for:

**IDEA**

✔ Unexplained reluctance to go to school.

✔ Fearfulness or unusual anxiety.

✔ Sleep disturbances and nightmares.

✔ Vague physical complaints (headaches, stomachaches), especially on school days.

✔ Clothes or other belongings that come home ripped or are missing altogether.

143

# What to Do if Your Kid is Being Bullied

Some parents may find it embarrassing to learn that their child is being bullied. As hard as it is to hear, we need to get over it! We need to support our kids when this is happening to them! A few simple tips when the subject of bullying comes up will make it a lot easier to deal with:

✔ **Be a good listener:**
Stay calm, and give your child plenty of time to tell you how he or she feels about the bully and the bullying. Avoid overly simplistic responses that discount your child's feelings. Saying things like, "Oh don't worry about it... that boy is just jealous" or "She was ridiculous to call you that name... just ignore her" may sound like good advice on the surface, but what children hear is that they are wrong to feel upset and the solution is so simple. Make it clear that being bullied is not your child's fault. Above all, don't just suggest your child fight back. Some kids are just non-aggressive by nature, and you can't make them change that (nor would you want to!).

✔
**Don't overreact – but make sure you do react:**
Ask yourself, how serious is this bullying? Is it serious enough to discuss with the teacher, with the principal, with the police? Don't just assume it's kid stuff, some sort of reaction is called for, but you need to think your response through. The best bet is to talk to the teacher first. Do it quickly, before the situation escalates. A "boys will be boys" type of response is unacceptable – don't succumb to pressures that have allowed bullying to persist in our schools for
✔ so long.

✔ **Help your child avoid the situations that expose him or her to bullying**

If the bullying is occurring on the way to or from school, find a safer route and arrange for an older child companion. Also, point out places the child can go for help when it happens. Finally, let the school authorities know when there is a problem, and keep a written record of incidents and who was involved.

When you're discussing the bullying with your child, keep in mind these tips to tell them:

✔ Being bullied is not their fault. This is the most important one!

✔ They don't have to face bullies on their own, there is help available.

✔ They can, with help, let bullies know that they are not afraid, and that they are determined to see that the bullying will stop.

✔ The school is aware of what is going on, and now that you know, you will make sure that things will get better.

✔ They did a good thing by telling you. There will always be things that they should never try to deal with on their own, and this is one of them.

If you suspect that bullying is occurring at your kid's school, you should ask the principal if it has an anti-bullying policy and, if it does, how well it works. If you're told that they don't have a bullying problem, don't buy it! The problem exists in all schools. School bullying is everyone's business, and while it is unrealistic to think that we can completely stop it, we can work to reduce it.

# I Think My Kid May be a Bully

**QUOTES**

> There is really no way to prevent bullying 100 percent. There will always be children, even ones raised in very tolerant and nurturing homes, who act out against their peers. However, if you want to significantly reduce the chances of your child becoming a bully, teach from the get-go. If you haven't had much focus on tolerance, even by age 4, it is never too late to start. Children are incredibly adaptive. Like hearty offshoots of trees, they soak up your family's values in the early years of child development, preschool and early elementary schools.
>
> Cheryl Murfin Bond,
> Editor-In-Chief, Washington's Child

There's always the possibility that you have the kid who is creating the problem. And while this may be embarrassing, remember that you have the tools necessary to change your child's behavior. During your family meals and meetings you can work these tips from for curbing or preventing bullying into your discussions:

1) **Respect children's troubles by acknowledging when they become targets of bias.** Don't minimize the experience. Provide emotional support and then brainstorm constructive responses. Develop a set of "comebacks" for children who are victims of name-calling. A healthy use of humor can sometimes diffuse even the most difficult situations.

2) **Read books with multicultural and tolerance themes to your children.** Assess the cultural diversity reflected in your home's artwork, music and literature. Add something new. Give multicultural doll, toys, and games as gifts.

3) **Point out stereotypes and cultural misinformation** depicted in movies, TV shows, computer games and other media. Don't pass any opportunity to challenge bias when it comes from friends and family members. Begin with a qualified statement: "Andrew just called people of XYZ faith 'lunatics.' What do you think about that, Zoë? How would you feel if someone called you that?" Let children do most of the talking.

4) **When a child says or does something that reflects biases or embraces stereotypes, point it out:** "What makes that joke funny, Jerome?" Guide the conversation toward internalization of empathy and respect: "Mimi uses a walker, honey. How do you think she would feel about that joke?" or "How did you feel when Robbie made fun of your glasses last week?"

5) **Look critically at how a child defines "normal." Expand the definition.** Visit playgrounds where a variety of children are present – people of different races/ethnicities, socioeconomic backgrounds, family structures, etc. Encourage a child to spend time with elders – grandparents, for example. Attend religious services at a variety of houses of worship.

6) **The earlier children interact with the community, the better.** If a child is interested in stars, visit the local library, museum or planetarium. A child who is concerned about world hunger can volunteer at a local soup kitchen or homeless shelter.

7) **Do not tell children that we are all the same; we're not.** We experience the world in different ways, and those experiences matter. Help your child understand the viewpoints of others.

Adapted From The Southern Poverty Law Center

As dedicated parents and as our children's primary role models, we need to be consistent in how we treat others and in our commitment to tolerance. Bullies usually tend to pick on people they can classify as "others" and if we parents treat people differently based on characteristics such as race or gender, our children are likely to do the same. But if we show them how to treat people fairly, and exercise that in our everyday lives, it's a good bet that our kids will do the same.

Watching your children become miserable because of bullying or teasing is emotionally torturous for parents. Sometimes our desire to lash out at others who hurt our children leads to emotionally driven and poorly thought-out responses (like picking an argument with the bully's parents). It is important for us to acknowledge the pain of seeing our children suffer and then focus on modeling appropriate responses, teaching helpful coping behaviors, and finding effective solutions.

**WARNING**

Besides the examples and ideas adapted from the Southern Poverty Law Center literature that we listed above, there are also some common-sense rules you can lay down for your kids to reduce the chances that they will be involved in bullying behaviors. Make your kids follow these four rules, both inside and outside the home, and have clear-cut consequences for them when they don't:

- ✔ **No insults**
- ✔ **No name calling**
- ✔ **No pushing**
- ✔ **No hitting**

It's important that kids see that everyone, especially their parents, is following the same rules. And when they break the rules they need to know that they will face consistent consequences every single time. The consequences need to be thought through ahead of time to make sure that they are reasonable and understood by everyone in the family.

The "Golden Rule" is still one of the most important lessons we can teach our children: Always treat others as you would want them to treat you.

# Teasing

Teasing is different from bullying; however, it is probably even more common, and definitely as harmful as bullying. Just to give you an example, being teased about physical appearance (one of the most common forms of teasing) has been shown to be a distinct factor in the development of eating disorders. Some of the tips for dealing with teasing are similar to those for dealing with bullying, but the most important thing we can do is to constantly bolster our children's self-esteem and work with them on practicing appropriate responses when they find themselves the victim of teasing. You should also take the same steps in alerting school officials about teasing that you would take in bullying instances.

> Our family continually emphasizes that we NEVER make fun of people's physical characteristics.

**WARNING**

# School Issues Exercise

**Step 1:** It's time to role-play! Each family member writes down (or verbally describes) an incident that occurred at school or work that was upsetting.

> **Big Hint #1:** This could be an incident in which a child was teased or bullied, a difficult interaction with a teacher, or an adult's disagreement with a coworker.

**Step 2:** The family members then decide who will play the roles of each person involved in the situation.

**Step 3:** First, they act out what actually happened until they get it just right. Then, the family members take turns acting out different ways that the situation could be handled.

**REMEMBER**

> **Big Hint #2: Don't be afraid to get a little goofy here, because sometimes laughter is the best way for a child to get over a bad experience. However, make sure that the laughter is not belittling the emotions the child feels as a result of the situation being discussed.**

**Step 4:** Each possibility is acted out and the family discusses the positive and negative aspects of each scenario. The person who was in the real situation at school or work can then make a plan of action for similar events in the future.

## What Have We Learned?

After reading this chapter, you should better understand some of the problems your kids may be experiencing at school. You've got some tools to help your kids through some rough spots, and you should be thinking about some of the signs we discussed that would show you your kid is having a problem at school.

You can also feel good about the fact that if you actually do the exercises you just read about you'll have an easily accomplished, structured way to talk to your kids about problems at school.

# Chapter Ten
# Friends and
# Peer Pressure

## Dealing With Friends
## and Peer Pressure

> "Associate yourself with men of good quality if you esteem
> your own reputation; for `tis better to be alone than in bad
> company."
>
> George Washington

**QUOTES**

Although the main focus of this book is on how to better connect with
your own family, you can see that the whole idea of family meals and
meetings is really bigger than that – it really provides you with a basis
from which to influence all the different parts of the lives of your
children. The lessons you teach at home, the things your children learn
around your family table, will be the lessons that your children bring
out into the world with them. However, as your children approach
adolescence, you'll find that your children's friends may seem to have
as much influence on them as you do – and quite often, more!

The good news is that research on this shows that peers are only more
influential on certain things like music and fashion. Children's main
values and beliefs continue to mirror their parents, much more so than
their friends. So, if you've been doing your best all along to pass along
your values, you should be okay. But it never hurts to continue to
remain vigilant, and keep an eye on just what peer groups your kids

may be finding themselves in.

One of the best ways to make sure that the influence of friends on your children is a positive factor is to equip your children with the proper tools and information to make the right choices when selecting friends. You may be surprised how early in your children's development you will need to start thinking about this.

Strong friendships formed in childhood are in many ways a sort of primer for intimacy in long-term relationships and marriage in adulthood. It's not too much of a stretch to figure out that friendless children can become friendless adults. So, getting your kids off on the right foot when it comes to making and maintaining friendships may just have an effect on the way they behave in relationships for the rest of their lives. Unless they learn when they're kids, they may never learn how to be a friend or how to get one. I know it all sounds pretty devastating, but don't worry – there are ways you can help!

# Let's Start at the Very Beginning

"Two are better than one; because they have a good reward for their labor. For if they fall, the one will lift up his fellow: but woe to him that is alone when he falleth; for he hath not another to help him up."

Ecclesiastes 4:9

**TOGETHER**

Just what is a healthy friendship? What are the hallmarks to look for in the relationships that your children are building outside the house? Carlen Henington, Ph.D., of Mississippi State University offers this definition of the elements of friendship:

## Elements of Friendship

✔ **Mutual affection and regard as demonstrated by an exchange of caring and a sense of responsibility for the other.**

✔ **Investment of time and attention through shared interests and activities.**

✔ **Commitment to the friendship and expectation that it will last across time.**

✔ **Reciprocal loyalty to the other's interests.**

✔ **Self-disclosure that fosters mutual understanding.**

✔ **Equality of power in the relationship.**

**FUN FACT**

This all seems simple enough, and looks like something everyone can

agree on. What Dr. Henington is saying is that friends should like each other, enjoy some of the same things, commit to each other, be loyal and truthful and neither friend should be the dominant one in the relationship. Sounds wonderful, I'll take a dozen!

But how do we get our children to the point where they can build relationships like that?

Well, we don't have to worry about it much for the first three years of our kids' lives because that's when they focus on forming secure attachments to their parents and other family members. But from the age of about three and on, your children's playmates are their first forays into friendship.

Simply enough, for a child of three, the major requirement of a playmate is proximity. They have to be in the same room! But once your child is in the same room with other children, there are ways that you can help them be a good playmate – and, for kids, that's well on the way to developing friendships.

# How to Help Your Child be a Good Playmate

**IDEA**

✔ Make sure that the toys in the room are the right level of play for their ages. Any child will quickly lose interest if a toy task is either too easy or too difficult.

✔ Have enough toys available so that each child has at least one toy to play with. The surest way to get toddlers brawling and bawling is having only one toy to be shared by several children.

✔ Try and make sure that all the toys work. Trying to pull a truck that only has three wheels can be a highly frustrating experience for a young child, and when kids get frustrated they can act out.

✔ You don't have to spend a lot of money on this. You can go to the local dollar store in your neighborhood and pick up several plastic toys for less than five bucks. As long as you have enough of them for the kids that will be playing together, any age-appropriate toy is fine. Age appropriate meaning that the kids can understand the toys, and that they are safe for the children, with no small parts for younger kids.

There's really only one way that childhood friendships are formed, and that's through playing together. And even though such friendships during the preschool years are often short-lived, as kids go to different schools or move away, their importance in the social development of your child should not be underestimated. It's their first experience at making friends, and you can help it be a positive one by following the steps above.

# The Basis for Friendship Changes as Children Get Older

**REMEMBER**

Dr. Henington again provides us with some definitions of friendship, focusing on the changing nature of friendship, as kids get older:

✔ *Preschooler/kindergarten years:* Young children form friendships based on availability and playmates are considered friends. Children choose playmates who are in physical proximity and who are engaged in a desirable activity. Play episodes are relatively brief with frequent changes in play partners.

✔ *Early elementary school years:* Friendship becomes more of an agreement or contract between playmates, complete with responsibilities and expectations for an exchange of favors and expected duties (birthday parties, sharing treats, unity as opposed to loyalty). Play episodes are longer, but friendships may not be enduring.

✔ *Later elementary school years:* Expectations become more sophisticated during this age. These include expectations for loyalty, mutual understanding and support. Children of this age spend increasing amounts of time (usually in games and sports) with friends (nearly twice as much) and the influence that peers exert over one another increases proportionally.

✔ *Adolescence:* Friendships no longer center on contracts; rather they increasingly resemble the friendships of adults. Friendship is based on mutuality, intimacy, shared support and loyalty.

Carlen Henington, Ph.D., Peer Relationships
in Childhood A Guide for Educators

I think you can see from this excerpt from Dr. Henington's study, that emotional stakes are raised as kids grow older and develop deeper friendships. So let's look at how we can help our kids build deeper, positive friendships.

# How to Help Your Child be a Good Friend

> He who walks with the wise grows wise, but a companion of fools suffers harm.
>
> Proverbs 13:20

**QUOTES**

With our corporate moves over the years we have been blessed with forming wonderful friendships all over the country. Neal and I believe that relationships are very important and try to not only tell our kids about the gift of friends, but also to show them how important it is to have strong relationships that bring so much joy into your lives.

# Model Good friendships

> The example of friendship you provide has a bigger impact on your child's friendships than any lecture. Children who see their parents treat each other and their friends with kindness and respect have an advantage. Baking cookies for the new neighbor or offering a listening ear for an unhappy friend sends your child a powerful message.
>
> U.S. Department of Education, Office of Intergovernmental and Interagency Affairs, Helping Your Child through Early Adolescence

**FUN FACT**

157

Friendships will affect many areas of your kids' lives–their grades, how they spend their time, what clubs they join, what sports they play and how they behave in public places. Research has shown that kids who have trouble forming friendships are more likely to have low self-esteem, get bad grades, drop out of school, get involved in delinquent behavior and suffer from a range of psychological problems when they become adults. It is important to share with your kids that to have a good friend, you need to be a good friend.

Some of you may be worrying that your children's friends will become so influential in their lives that your own roles will diminish. Parents worry still more that their children's friends will encourage them to take part in harmful activities.

Middle-school is the time that most experts agree is the peak period for peer influence. During this time, friends often influence taste in music, clothes or hairstyles, as well as the activities in which youngsters choose to participate.  Don't get too freaked out by all of this:  peers do not and cannot replace parents. You are still the most important influence in your child's life.  All that discussion we had about being a good role model back in Chapter Seven will really pay off here!

Most experts agree that young teens are more inclined to turn to their parents than to peers for guidance in deciding what post-high-school plans to make, what career to select and what religious and moral values to choose.  This influence is greatest when the bond between parent and child is strong – and that's the bond you're strengthening every time you sit down to a family meal and meeting.

Here are some tips to guide you in helping your child to form good and healthy friendships:

**EXAMPLE**

✔ **Recognize that peer pressure can be bad or good.**
Most kids are drawn to friends who are similar to them. If your child chooses friends who are not interested in school and who

make poor grades, he may be less willing to study or complete assignments. If he chooses friends who like school and do well in their studies, his motivation to get good grades may be strengthened. Friends who avoid alcohol and drugs also will exert a positive influence on your child. We share with our kids that eagles soar with eagles, so surround yourself with kids that can make you the best person you can be and you do the same for them.

✔ **Get to know your child's friends.**

A good way to get to know your kid's friends is to drive them to events–talking with them in the car can reveal a lot about how they think about things. Silence is golden as well. It is amazing how you seem invisible when your kids and their friends are talking in the car!  Make sure that they feel welcome in your home – provide food and drinks and make it a comfortable atmosphere. Having your house as the neighborhood hangout can provide you with peace of mind (knowing where your child is) and allows you to set the rules of conduct. You'll also have a much better understanding of what they talk about, what their concerns are, and how they are really spending their time. It is our goal as parents of teens to make our home the house our kids' friends want to come to and our kids want to have their friends come to.  When I was growing up my house was like that. (It helped that my mom is probably the best cook in the world and that my dad is the funniest guy I know.) Our dinner table had guests added frequently. It was so common to come to the dinner table and have my mom or dad whisper to the family..."FHB", which meant "Family Hold Back", because we needed to make the food last! What a wonderful atmosphere it was to grow up in.

✔ **Get to know the parents.**

You don't have to become best buddies with the parents of your kid's friend, but you need to know if the parents' attitudes and approaches to parenting are similar to yours. The kid may seem okay, but you need to know if someone is around at the other house to supervise! Their rules may be stricter than yours, or they might just be totally off the wall! We learned this the tough way. A couple of years ago we picked up our son from a friend's house and there was a rifle perched up by the front door. To this day, whether our children are babysitting for a family or they are going over someone's house to play, we always ask if they have guns in the house. Knowing the other parents makes it easier to learn what you need to know about what your kids are doing with their friends: where your child is going, who they're going with, what time the activity starts and ends, whether an adult will be present and how your child will get to and from the activity. Most conscientious parents will welcome your overtures – if the parents are uncommunicative, you may want to think about discouraging the friendship.

✔ **Make sure your child has some down time in a safe place to hang around with friends.**
Too many piano lessons or basketball practices can lead to burnout. Allowing your kids some free time with friends in a safe place with adult supervision lets them share ideas and develop important social skills. For example, while hanging out with friends your child can learn that good friends are good listeners, that they are helpful and confident, that they are enthusiastic, possess a sense of humor and that they respect others. Spending time with others may also help your child to improve on some behaviors that make others uncomfortable around him: maybe your kid is too serious or unenthusiastic, critical of others or too stubborn. Basically, they need some time to be kids together, to help each other grow up.

✔ **Talk with your child about friends, about friendship and about making choices.**
It's completely normal for adolescents to worry about what the other kids think about them. This makes it especially important for

you to use your family meals and meeting times to talk with your kids about resisting the inevitable peer pressure to disobey the rules or go against the standards and values that you have taught them. Neal's father had a speech that he gave to Neal as he walked out of the house in high school…"I trust you will make the right choices." He told him there may be times when he is with friends and their choices may not be the right ones, so sometimes you just need to walk away! This really worked! Talk about what it takes to be a good friend and about how all friendships have their ups and downs. You can also talk about the importance of making good choices when they are with friends – tell them that if it feels wrong, it probably is.

✔ **Teach your child how to get out of a bad situation**
Talk with your kids about dangerous or inappropriate situations that might come up and explore possible ways to handle them. This is just like the role-playing exercise we did at the end of Chapter Nine. Ask your 14-year-old daughter what she would do if a guest arrived at a slumber party with a bottle of wine in her overnight bag? Ask your 12-year-old son how he would handle a suggestion from a friend to cut school and head for a nearby burger place? If you arm your kid with the right tools to get him or herself out of a tricky situation, they're more likely to make the right choices. We have a code we use with our kids. If they are in a situation and they feel they want to leave, they call us and say "I forgot to feed Gypsy, (our dog)." We immediately go and get them, wherever they are. And you can always tell them to make you the bad guy and say that their Mom says, "No!" or that their Dad would kill them.

✔ **Always Leave Them A Safety Net**
The biggest thing to always remember is that no child going out for an evening should be without change for a phone call, or the knowledge of how to make a collect call. They need to be able to call you, or the police, at anytime! As a last resort, this may literally

**REMEMBER**

be a lifeline. A cell phone is a great idea if you can afford one, and you teach your children how to use the phone responsibly.

**WARNING**

✔ **Keep an eye on things to help your child avoid risky and unhealthy behavior.**

No matter how responsible your kids may be, it's a fact that young adolescents need supervision, especially during the hours between school and dinner. Make sure that you keep up to date on exactly who your children's friends are and just what they're doing when they get together. Don't ever be embarrassed to be the nosy guy, or afraid to be the jerk who makes the phone call to the other parents' house to make sure that your kid is there, and that the parent is actually there and supervising. And don't ever be afraid to say no when you're unsure about the safety or appropriateness of a situation. Maybe your kid will hate you for a day or two, but if you let your kid do something that you didn't feel right about and something awful happens, you'll regret it for the rest of your life.

Experts disagree as to whether parents should try to stop their children from seeing a friend that the parents dislike. Some kids will rebel when they're told they can't spend time with certain friends. Well, you need to expect a certain amount of rebellion anyway, don't you? And doesn't someone need to be the parent in this relationship? I come down on the side with the experts who suggest that you should let your child know that you disapprove of a friendship and exactly why you disapprove. Let your kid know in no uncertain terms why you feel that a particular friendship may be harmful to them. Limit the amount of time and the activities that you will allow with the friend in question, have them do more together in your presence and steer your kid towards other activities.

# If All Your Friends Were Jumping Off a Cliff...

There's a very telling scene in a dark and macabre Wynona Rider comedy (definitely not for kids!) named Heathers, which offers a pretty bleak view on peer pressure. When the Wynona Rider character asks her best friend, "If all your friends were jumping off a cliff, would you jump also?" and her friend replies "Probably, " Wynona says, "Yeah, me too." That's a pretty simplistic, yet fairly common view of the peer pressure that kids face, but I'm here to tell you that it doesn't have to be that way.

If you continue to build on the core values of your family through family meals and meetings, and continue to follow the tips outlined in this book, you may actually guide your children into relationships where they receive positive peer pressure. The belief is that if you work as hard as you can to encourage your child to hang around with good kids, then they will push each other to succeed. And there's absolutely no reason why this cannot work.

**REMEMBER**

Children of all ages need to feel that they fit in – that they belong. As children approach the teen years, the need to be "one of the gang" becomes stronger than at any other age, before or after. Friendships become closer and more important and play a key part in allowing young adolescents to sort out who they are and where they're headed in life. They are likely to form small groups or cliques, each with a special identity (more on this later). I'm sure you remember how it was!

Some kids give in to peer pressure because they want to be liked, to fit in, or because they worry that other kids may make fun of them if they don't go along with the group. This is where your hard work at providing a role model and increasing family communication will help your child in making the right decisions. We firmly believe that with a proper grounding in your own particular family values, your child will have a stronger foundation from which they can resist peer pressure.

Others kids may go along with peer pressure because they are curious to try something new that others are doing. The idea that "everyone's doing it" may influence some kids to leave their better judgment, or their common sense, behind.  This is where all the work you've put into monitoring your kids activities and making sure they have proper supervision will help your kids make the right choices.  If you know where your kids are, and what they are doing, it is much less likely that when they do make their inevitable errors in judgment that those errors will not be devastating ones.

**QUOTES**

"The fact is, peer pressure can be positive. It keeps youth participating in religious activities, going to 4-H meetings and playing on sports teams, even when they are not leaders. It keeps adults going to religious services, serving on community committees and supporting worthwhile causes. The peer group is a source of affection, sympathy and understanding; a place for experimentation…it is no wonder, then, that adolescents like to spend time with their peers."

Herbert G. Lingren, Extension Family
Scientist, University of Nebraska

Remember that peers can have a positive influence on each other. Maybe another student in your kid's science class taught them an easy way to remember the planets in the solar system.  Or perhaps someone on the soccer team showed them how to do a cool trick with the ball. They might admire a friend who always exhibits good sportsmanship and try to be more like her. Maybe your kid got others excited about her new favorite book, and now everyone's reading it. These are all examples of how peers can positively influence each other everyday. One of the best compliments we have received was from a parent that told us what a great influence Kyle was on their son! It doesn't get any better than that!

Finally, if we really work on the aspects of family communication that we discussed in Chapter Six, specifically the bits about teaching your children an assertive communication style, there should be little worry about negative peer pressure at all. With the values you're imparting at your family meals and meetings, and the ability to openly and honestly communicate just what they're feeling, it will be your kid that will be setting the standards for their peer groups!

# Understanding the Teen "Class" Structure

One phenomenon that has become more prominent in the adolescent social structure, certainly more so today than when I was growing up, is the need for young adults to band together in "cliques."

At this age, children are becoming adults and are desperately searching for their self-identity. All the while, raging hormones and the other problems inherent to this age become more and more apparent – creating a need to "fit in." Ironically, the teens typically feel that they are "all alone."

This tends to lead to a sort of social structure where children band together with groups most like themselves. Even so-called "loners" band together with other loners. The strangest of this behavior is exemplified when teens change their hair to some odd color (such as purple) in order to "be different..." – meanwhile all of their immediate friends have done the same thing.

Here are some examples of different social "groups" common to teens:

✔ **Preps:** Preps are often seen as teens whose parents are upper-middle class, and otherwise well off financially. Quite often, they are the first to have nice cars, wear nice clothes, and be popular. However, success breeds contempt, and therefore, those not in this clique often are envious and/or spiteful. The stereotype of the rich kids hosting a party while their parents are away is sadly, all too true. So if your child should be in this loose category, you should be certain of their plans, and exactly what type of friends they are hanging out with. Far too often, this group holds wolves in sheep's clothing. These kids tend to be the ones with the disposable money to buy the drugs!

✔ **Jocks:** It is easy to conjure up pictures of the All-American Football Hero when thinking of this category. And while football is certainly one category, any school athletic group is bound to cause camaraderie. The competitive nature of sports, however, can lead to some problems if not tempered. It is important that by the time your child, should they be athletically inclined, is well-schooled in the importance of fair play and good sportsmanship.

✔ **Geeks:** Perhaps one of the saddest facets of being a teenager is their capacity for cruelty. The "smart" kids, along with the less than brilliant, the not-so-pretty, and generally anyone different than the so-called "norm" are often lumped into the "Geek" group. This group is often the subject of ridicule and/or resentment. For mutual protection, children in this category will quite often form friendships, only reinforcing the stereotype. Teens who might be labeled "geeks, freaks, nerds, weirdos, etc." are prone to bouts of depression, self-loathing and other negative emotions. It is important that they be encouraged and nurtured through this difficult period. Ironically, it is from this group that most of the future leaders and pillars of the community come.

✔ **Ethnic Groups:** Different ethnic groups, especially children who are not native English speakers, find themselves banding together. Similar ideologies, cultures and even languages create a bond that helps them cope with what otherwise is seen as a "foreign" situation, together.

✔ **Goths:** Goths are a rather new sort of classification given birth by the morbid messages being preached by so much of today's music and other mediums. The feelings of depression often manifest in wearing dark clothing, odd coloring of hair, painted fingernails and dark makeup (even among boys). Bouts of depression and even self-mutilation are not uncommon, and strangely considered "cool." Although this group is about the depression of not fitting in, this is perhaps among the most dangerous expression of lashing out at the angst of being a teenager. Understanding and patience is crucial.

✔ **Good Ol' Boys:** 4H membership, shop class, cowboy hats and boots are all common for this group of teens. Regardless of what part of the country you're in, there are inevitably going to be teens in this group. While this can be among the most pleasant group of well-meaning kids, it is also a group that glamorizes underage drinking and wild behavior.

✔ **Troublemakers:** Though never seen as a group, troublemaking teens rarely act alone. If your child is a troublemaker, the signs are obvious. Skipping classes, acting out in class and disorderly behavior are all symptoms. All too often, this can stem from actions of their so-called friends and peers.

✔ **Loners:** This is the most difficult "grouping" to peg. These are self-absorbed, shy or introverted teens. Whether by choice or as a defense mechanism, they for some reason spend most of their time brooding by themselves. Encourage your teen to become more involved if they exhibit this behavior. You should also try to find out exactly WHY they are acting the way they are.

**REMEMBER**

None of these classifications are pretty or flattering – and certainly nobody likes to be categorized. Unfortunately, that's precisely what teens across America are doing every day.

Also, don't expect your children to use these titles or categories. They're rarely even aware that they're even segmenting themselves. Quite often the lines between groups blur. Preps may be Jocks as well as Troublemakers. Geeks may be Goths or Loners. Or there may be categories not even represented by the list above.

It is worth knowing that this sort of "class" or "segmentation" does exist and to encourage your own children to look past the classification. Good, real, and lasting friendships can be forged regardless of how someone dresses, or what they have piercing their nose. And a missed friendship could be an awful thing indeed.

Neal and I were really moved recently when we attended the high school freshman orientation that Caitlin helped put on. They played the song "True Colors" by Cindi Lauper while the kids pantomimed the stereotyping of the different groups mentioned above, ignoring and judging each other. As the song ended, the kids came together with the help of two kids from two different groups, like a modern day West Side Story! It was a great message.

**EXAMPLE**

# Exercises for Dealing With Friends and Peer Pressure

Here are a few exercises you can try at your family meal and meeting to reinforce what you've read in this chapter:

## "The Friend-Ship"

**Step One:** Each family member makes a "friend-ship." At the top of the ship, each family member should list the names of their five best friends in a row.

**Step Two**: Below each name, the family member lists three positive characteristics of each of the friends and three negative characteristics.

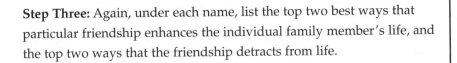

**Big Hint #1: Let everyone know that this is to be kept private among the family members, as others may be unnecessarily hurt by the discussion, if they were to hear parts of it out of context of the whole exercise.**

**WARNING**

**Step Three:** Again, under each name, list the top two best ways that particular friendship enhances the individual family member's life, and the top two ways that the friendship detracts from life.

**Step Four:** Discuss each other's "friend-ship" in depth. This will help you and your kids really understand how and why you're friends with certain people, and will clearly point out which are the relationships they should pursue further and which are the relationships that perhaps they should be spending less time on.

## "How to Be a Better Friend"

**Step One:** For each family member, the group makes a list of the characteristics that make the individual a really good friend.

**TOGETHER**

**Step Two:** Now, the group lists all of the individual's characteristics that may make it difficult to be friends with them.

**Step Three:** Finally, in light of all of the feedback, the family discusses constructive suggestions regarding how each family member can be an even better friend.

## "I Trust You!"

**Step One:** The spirit of cooperation and trust are important parts of building lasting relationships. This exercise further develops those skills.

**REMEMBER**

> **Big Hint #1: This is a lot of fun, but it can also be very messy. It would be a good idea to wear old t-shirts and to lay large garbage bags or plastic on the floor.**

**Step Two:** Break the family breaks down into teams of two. If there are an uneven number of people, one individual can serve as judge/timekeeper. If there is an even number of people, one team will perform at a time.

**Step Three:** Both members of the team are blindfolded. One team member will serve as the feeder and the other will be the eater. The feeder is handed a spoon and cup of chocolate pudding … you can substitute applesauce, yogurt, or any other food that's kind of gooey and potentially messy!

**Step Four:** The goal is for the feeder to successfully get the food into the eater's mouth. The team is timed and time is called when the cup is empty. The team members then switch places and repeat the exercise. The best time of the two trials is used to decide the winners.

> **Big Hint #2: The team members can give each other suggestions to improve their chance of success, such as "That's my chin, move the spoon up!"**

**Step Five:** After the winners are announced and a pre-determined prize is awarded, discuss what led to the victory. Explore the types of communication successes and failures, the thoughts, and the feelings that led to the more successful partnerships as well as the less successful ones.

## What Have We Learned?

After reading this chapter, you should better understand some of the ways that you can help your kids develop healthy and productive friendships and garner some positive influences from their peers. You've got some tips and tools to help guide your kids into friendships that will help them grow into well-adjusted adults, and you should be thinking about some of the ways we discussed to help you determine if your kids are indeed developing the kind of healthy relationships we would all prefer.

You should also feel good about the fact that if you actually do the exercises you just read about you'll have a simple and structured way to talk to your kids about dealing with friend and peer pressure.

# Chapter Ten

# Chapter Eleven
## Family Faith

## Faith Issues and Spiritual Growth

> "Churches, temples and mosques are well-positioned to cultivate anti-drug values and teach effective coping skills for dealing with peer pressure and stress. Instilling strong values, rooted for many in religious faiths, helps prevent teen marijuana use and other risky behaviors."
>
> Jim Towey, Director of the White House Office of Faith-Based and Community Initiatives

**QUOTES**

Neal and I have committed ourselves to a Christian lifestyle, and as a result of that we are raising our children as Christians. The Dunns are raising their family in the Jewish faith. We both feel these are the right choices for us, and to offer our children a value system rooted in faith-based beliefs is the best start in life we can offer them. We realize that people believe in many different faiths, and we applaud their efforts to raise their children in accordance with the tenets of the particular faith they have been called to, or have chosen.

The point here is that we believe children need to be raised with a basic grounding in some sort of faith – even if that faith is based only on having good morals. Children need a belief system to help them build strong values and morals. Whatever faith, sect or denomination you choose for your family is fine, and we urge you to share your faith with your children completely.

So, please remember as you read this chapter, that although I may be coming from a Christian perspective or bias, we feel the things we discuss in this chapter are applicable to any faith that you choose to follow and that you choose to instruct your children in.

I have an example from the Bible that I feel illustrates the importance of grounding children within a faith. Many of you may be familiar with the parable of the sower and the seed in the thirteenth chapter of Matthew's Gospel. In that story, the good soil was essential for the seed to grow into what God intended. This is also true of our children. As parents, there are many areas over which I have no control. However, I can create the very best soil for my children to grow in. Without strong roots in rich soil, they will not have the foundation to become the wonderful people that God intended. We have discovered that eating family meals and conducting family meetings together makes for good soil and allows the roots of communication and trust to grow deep and strong.

Churches, synagogues, and other places of worship provide a wonderful forum for social interaction for the whole family. With a wholesome environment, friendly atmosphere and structured activities, this can often prove to develop good communication and interpersonal skills.

# Is it Your Responsibility to Help Your Children Grow in Their Faith?

> "Parents typically have no plan for the spiritual development of their children; do not consider it a priority, have little or no training in how to nurture a child's faith, have no related standards or goals that they are seeking to satisfy, and experience no accountability for their efforts."
> Barna Research Group, www.barna.org

**QUOTES**

The Barna Research Group, Ltd. is an independent marketing research company located in southern California. Since 1984, it has been studying cultural trends related to values, beliefs, attitudes and behaviors.

A recent Barna study found that:

✔ 85% of parents of children under age 13 believe they have the primary responsibility for teaching their children about religious beliefs and spiritual matters.

**FUN FACT**

✔ 11% said their church is primarily responsible.

✔ 1% said it is mostly the domain of their child's school.

✔ Just a few parents assigned such responsibility to friends, society or the media.

Barna also found that nearly all parents of children under the age of 13 – 96% – believe that they have the primary responsibility for teaching their children values. Just 1% said their church has that task and 1% assigned that role to the child's school.

That all sounds just about right to me. And I'm happy that so many people understand that they have the responsibility to instruct their kids in spiritual matters and teach them, their family values. But it's the related research from Barna that gives me cause for concern.

Barna found that a majority of parents do not spend any time during a typical week discussing religious matters or studying religious materials with their children. However, about two out of three parents of children 12 or younger attend religious services at least once a month and generally take their children with them. Most of those parents are willing to let their church or religious center provide all of the direct religious teaching and related religious experiences that their children receive.

I believe that we all need to go further than that, and that teaching your children faith based relationship principles helps families not only become more skillful and confident in their communications but will also create spiritual bonds that last a lifetime.

# How to Help Your Children Grow in Their Faith

QUOTES

"Public schools may teach the history of religion, comparative religion, scripture-as-literature, and the role of religion in the history of the United States and other countries. Similarly, it is permissible to consider religious influences on art, music, literature, and social studies. Students may also express their beliefs about religion in the form of homework, artwork, and other written and oral assignments. Such work should be judged by ordinary academic standards of substance and relevance, however, and not based on the religious content. Although public schools may teach about religious holidays, including their religious aspects, and may celebrate the secular aspects of holidays, schools may not observe holidays as religious events or promote such observance by students."

National PTA, *A Parent's Guide to Religion in the Public Schools*

I'm not suggesting that our Catholic friends need to launch directly into deep theological discussions about the transubstantiation of the Eucharist, or that our Muslim friends need to crack open the Mufradat of Raghib (dictionary of the Holy Qu'ran) every night at the dinner table. There is obviously a reason why we'll always need some of us to go to seminaries and divinity schools! What I am suggesting is that, as parents, all of us need to discuss with our kids how our belief systems affect our view of simple, easier to grasp topics, like the Ten Commandments. Unless you're paying the money to send your kids to a faith-based school, they're certainly not learning about the Ten Commandments in public schools!

**QUOTES**

Churches only get one or two hours a week with these children. Parents have them for many hours each week and experience numerous opportunities to teach the kids vital principles in a range of settings and situations. The more intentional a church is about giving parents the confidence and the tools to raise up spiritual champions, the more effective we found the congregation's parents to be as spiritual mentors.

George Barna, *Transforming Children into Spiritual Champions*

Here's an easy and fun way to teach your children about the concept of faith, adapted from *52 Faith Building Activities* by Paul and Rebecca Armstrong:

Faith is defined as the substance of things hoped for, the evidence of things not seen. (Heb 11:1) We can have a hope that is sure and certain, because faith has substance and evidence. Children easily understand faith, and we believe in God because, although we don't see Him now, we do see profound evidence of His loving influence in our lives.

To do this exercise, you'll need a pillow case, and three or four familiar objects, such as a teddy bear, a cup, a bell, and a book. Gather these familiar objects that can be identified easily by touch or sound alone, and put them into the pillow case.

**EXAMPLE**

**Step 1:** Instruct your child to put his or her hand into a pillowcase (without looking). Can they guess what the objects are?

**Step 2:** Ask your child to explain why they think it's a teddy bear (for example). They may answer, "It's fluffy," "It has a button nose," or "I recognize the corner of the ear that the dog chews on." Explain that these things are called "evidence." This evidence makes it easy to believe they've grabbed a teddy bear. Take a look. Did your child guess correctly?

**Step 3:** What did your child grab next? What do they think it is? What evidence do they have? Explain that we have faith when we gather all the "evidence" and make a decision without really seeing what happened or what the object is. Repeat the activity a couple of times.

**Step 4:** Wrap up the game by explaining we have faith in God, whom we can't see – but we know God is real, because our faith has evidence. Ask, "How do you know God is real? What evidence do you have that God loves you?" (Be sure to keep things light and fun).

This is a simple and fun way to explain the concept of faith to your children, and as you can see, it will work no matter what religion your family is affiliated with.

You can also begin to build faith and spiritual growth by giving your children opportunities during your family meals and meeting to discuss what God means to them. This will be a good preparation for them to be able to express and live their faith outside of regular church services. Provide time each week for at least one child to share what God has done for him or her. Ask them to think about what we can thank God for today.

This is also a good time to share your family meals and meetings with significant friends and relatives, or you can invite members from your congregation to come to your house to share their testimonies. This will inspire the children and help them learn through the example of familiar adult and teen role models.

# Why Do We Have to go to Services All the Time?

**QUOTES**

"The right and duty of parents to give education is essential, since it is connected with the transmission of human life; it is original and primary with regard to the educational role of others, on account of the uniqueness of the loving relationship between parents and children; and it is irreplaceable and inalienable, and therefore incapable of being entirely delegated to others or usurped by others."

> Holy Father's Apostolic Exhortation,
> *The Role of the Christian Family in the Modern World (Familiaris Consortio)*

I'm sure you've heard the kids complain about going to services from time to time – maybe even you or your spouse sometimes raised the question of why you need to go all the time, when you're feeling a little sleepy and looking for a reason not to go to services.

Many people say that they can worship God just as well, if not better, by digging in their garden or riding their surfboard. They think there must be a better way to praise God than by sitting in some stuffy old building. In one sense they are right, for God is not specifically looking for people who pray in a formal house of worship. Going to religious services, praying, reading scripture, donating money to charities – these are all good things to do, but they do not necessarily make us better people. That needs to come from the lessons and values you're imbedding around the family table.

As for attending religious services, it will become more natural for your kids once they realize that they are all in God's family. At that point, they would want to meet with other members of the family. For example, the Bible describes the church as a meeting of believers who gather to encourage and build up one another by prayer, hearing the Bible read and taught, using their gifts, and serving one another in love. When these kinds of activities happen, going to religious services will be a positive experience. Attending religious services, like scripture reading, prayer, and acts of kindness, does not produce faith, but is the product of faith.

In our home, it isn't an option. Going to church and practicing our faith is who we are and what we do. It may be different for you. Until the time comes that your kids can *really* understand why they are going to services, maybe it's enough —when combined with parental teaching about religion and values – that you just make sure your kids get into the *habit* of going.

If time is an issue, many houses of worship have begun offering a variety of services. Choosing a time that works best for your family's schedule may help with any time problems your family may be facing.

# The Home is the Domestic Church

From the beginning of the church, the family home was considered a holy and sacred place for prayer, worship and ritual. The hearth and the family table were the domestic shrines for celebration and storytelling. Mothers and fathers and grandparents presided. When the early Christians assembled in their homes to proclaim scripture and celebrate Eucharist, they affirmed the sanctity of the home and validated the words of Jesus: "Where two or three are gathered in my name, I am in their midst." .... During the first centuries of Christianity, the family with its ordinary events and home celebrations exemplified the characteristics of the larger, universal Church.

> Rita Waldref, cited by Vincent Penderghest,
> Family Minister, St. Patrick's and St. Lawrence
> Parishes, in The Domestic Church

There is a growing awareness of the concept of the home as the domestic church, as a place that can supplement the teachings of your chosen faith on a daily basis. Religious leaders of all faiths are realizing that each community is essential for the other. Parishes simply cannot exist without families that people them and provide them with their unique personalities. Families, on the other hand, need their religious community to help them connect with a story of faith and commitment that is broader than their own experience.

The domestic church, the church at home, is not complete of itself. It should be united with and supported by the parishes and other communities within the larger church. It is the mission of the larger faith to which you belong to bring the smaller domestic churches together on days of worship, so that you can all share in your faith as a community. Hopefully, each family returns home nourished and renewed by the word and the services -- ready to live their faith in their day-to-day lives. Neither the local church nor the domestic church can complete its mission without the other. They need each other for their existence.

Unfortunately, although the idea of the domestic church is spreading, the reaction of some churches shows that organized religion isn't really keeping up their end of the deal. According to the Barna survey we discussed earlier, only one out of every five parents of children under 13 (19%) has ever been personally contacted or spoken to by a church leader to discuss the parents' involvement in the spiritual life and development of their youngsters.

You can change that by your own actions. Seek out your spiritual advisors and let them know that you're interested in the idea of a domestic church, for the purpose of strengthening your children's faith, and ask for the help and support of the church. If you are rebuffed, or ignored, maybe it's time to seek new spiritual advisors!

In the meantime, you can create an atmosphere of domestic church in your home in several different ways:

✔ One of the simplest ways is to ask a different family member to say a grace, or a blessing, before you begin any one of your family meals or meetings.

✔ Lighting candles before a meal or any other sort of family ritual can add to the atmosphere of a domestic church.

**EXAMPLE**

✔ Encouraging your children to say their prayers every night before they go to sleep is another way.

✔ If your family does not pray, then you can just encourage your children to think about all the things they are thankful for, every night before they go to sleep.

**IDEA**

# Exercises for Faith and Spiritual Growth

Here's an exercise you can do to explore just how your family views its faith, and what aspects of that faith are most important to the individual family members.

**Step #1:** Imagine that your family was on a cruise when a freak accident left you stranded on a remote desert island with fifty of your shipmates. There is little hope for rescue within the next six months, but you will have plenty of food and supplies to survive for at least one year.

**Step #2:** In trying to create a temporary civilization, the group divides responsibilities and appoints your family to be in charge of the island's religious/spiritual activities.

**REMEMBER**

Big Hint #1: Don't reject any of the kids' suggestions right off the bat. The whole idea here is to explore exactly how they view religion, your faith, their role in it, and what they hope to get out of the entire experience.

**Step #3:** You need to start a new religion! As a family, discuss:

**Discussion Point #1:** What are your priorities in taking on the role of spiritual leaders?

**Discussion Point #2:** What are the core beliefs and values that will characterize your spiritual leadership?

**Discussion Point #3:** What are the goals for religious education of children on the island?

**Discussion Point #4:** What are your ideas for creating a house of worship?

**Discussion Point #5:** What are the religious norms and rituals that you would like to create?

# What Have We Learned?

After reading this chapter, you should better understand some of the ways that you can help your kids develop a healthy faith and encourage spiritual growth. You've got some tips and tools to help guide your kids into following a faith that will help them develop a system of values by which to direct their lives. You should also be thinking about how you can better shoulder some of the responsibility that you as a parent have for helping to plant the seeds of a faith that will last a lifetime for your children.

You should also feel good about the fact that if you actually do the exercises you just read about you'll have an easily accomplished, simple and structured way to talk to your kids about faith and spiritual growth issues.

# Chapter Eleven

# Chapter Twelve
## Food, Eating, and Body Image Issues

## Food and Eating

> "Wish I had time for just one more bowl of chili."
>
> Last words of Kit Carson,
> American frontiersman (1809-1868)

QUOTES

As we're all working towards the goal of having more family meals and meetings, we should also be thinking about the basic thing that is happening at the table: eating. How many kids and adults today have bad eating habits that can lead to poor health and eating disorders? In this chapter I'd like to focus on healthy eating habits, and how to make them part of your kids' everyday life.

We all know many of the basic differences between "healthy" or "nutritious" foods and foods that are considered "unhealthy" or "treats." Most of us have been exposed to the food pyramids that teach us to eat plenty of fruits, vegetables, whole grains, and some protein, and to avoid eating too many sugars and fats. This way of eating seems to make common sense and many of us strive to follow it. Although many adults are now adopting high protein, low carbohydrate diets to lose weight, where our kids are concerned the goal should be eating a variety of healthy foods from each of the main food groups.

Unfortunately, it's just not that easy for parents to get the kids to eat what and how much we would like. Children have minds, taste buds, hunger and fullness signals of their own that direct their eating behavior. And despite what many parents think, this is a good thing! We should want our children to learn to respond to their internal signals of hunger and fullness and recognize the variety of tastes that appeal to them.

**QUOTES**

> "In America, a parent puts food in front of a child and says, 'Eat it, it's good for you.' In Europe, the parent says, 'Eat it. It's good!'"
>
> John Bainbridge, *Another Way of Living*

# Common Misconceptions About Eating

✔ **My chiid needs a lot of food to grow and be healthy**
Not so! Your child only needs enough of the right nutrients to grow properly. American portions have grown out of control! Our concept of what a full meal is actually represents *overeating* much of the time. It's important to remember that kids have relatively small stomachs and do not need as much as we think they do to be full or to be nourished. Don't push quantity; sometimes a little bit goes a long way. Focus on teaching your children to enjoy a little bit of a variety of nutritious foods.

✔ **If I don't push him/her to eat, my child will wilt away.**
It may seem that way, but studies prove otherwise. Without direction, kids may exhibit some strange eating patterns (like eating only one food for several days, rejecting foods of a particular color or texture, etc.), but they will end up eating

enough food for appropriate weight gain and acceptable nutrition if a variety of foods are available. In other words, they won't starve themselves! Now this doesn't mean that we can just let the kids do all the meal planning, but it does mean that you can cut back on nagging, begging, negotiating, and threatening your kids into eating. Regular check-ups at the pediatrician's office will include measuring your child's growth and usually will calm your fears. Also, kids' appetites can vary a great deal. Although they may not eat much on one particular day, they are likely to eat more on another day. So we can all calm down a little bit – by the end of the week things usually balance out.

✔ **If I don't give them candy, my kids won't learn to desire it.**
Not true! Children naturally desire foods that are sweet. Although we have to develop a taste for many vegetables and meats, we seem to have no problem enjoying ice cream or candy from the first moment they cross our lips. It is true that if you never exposed children to any treats they wouldn't know to ask for them, but when they see other kids eating stuff you have avoided, at the first opportunity they will taste them. Despite your efforts, they will like them and then they will want more.

# Some of the Silly Things We Say

✔ **Don't play with your food!**
Letting kids fully experience the texture, combined tastes, and possible games they can play with food may foster positive feelings about eating. I can still remember my father's famous pea trick in which he kept a pea suspended in the air by leaning his head back, balancing a pea on his lips and lightly blowing on it. I wasn't wild about the taste of peas, but the sight of them on my

**MEAL TIME**

plate signaled that we were in for some fun. Broccoli is just tiny trees begging to be planted in the mashed potatoes and green beans are so much more fun when you go searching for the tiny baby beans inside! Although you don't want to let the playing get out of hand, some healthy exploration and enjoyment with the food on your child's plate can be a good thing.

✔ **There are children starving in Africa! How can you leave all of that food on your plate?**
I can still remember asking my mother for an envelope whenever she said this! Using guilt by referring to starvation in a faraway land is rarely an effective technique. It's nice to teach your children to appreciate the bounty of food you have made available to them, but avoid the unintended suggestion that their wastefulness is directly connected to world hunger.

✔ **You can't leave the table until you clean your plate.**
Kids should stop eating when their stomachs feel full. When we demand that our children eat all of their food, we are teaching them to ignore their internal cues of fullness to meet external demands. Overriding their natural system in this way can have long-term negative consequences. It teaches them to overeat. Yes, there are times when children falsely proclaim "I'm full" because they don't like what they are eating or want to get back to the TV or some other activity, and that is okay. There will be natural consequences for faking fullness, like being really hungry later when the food is all put away and *no snacking is allowed*.

✔ **If you behave well now, you can have a hot fudge sundae later.**
It seems so innocent (and it works) to promise treats as rewards. But we must resist the temptation of bribing or rewarding our children with desserts. These days even pediatrician's offices are offering stickers instead of the symbolic lollipop for a good appointment. Part of developing a healthy attitude towards food and eating is not *equating* food with love, approval, comfort, and

reward. We often celebrate with food – birthday cakes, dinner celebrations after graduation or starring in the school play, and Thanksgiving and other holiday feasts are the norm. The overall experience ought to be that getting together with family and friends for togetherness and enjoying good food together is a joyous occasion. The focus need not be *solely* on the food.

# Parental Role Modeling

> "Eat not to dullness; drink not to elevation."
> Ben Franklin, American Statesman

**QUOTES**

Ask any adult about what their family eating patterns were as they grew up and you'll proceed to take a long stroll down food memory lane. There will be talk of favorite homemade foods that are missed, jokes about awful dishes and dreaded combinations, cherished food and eating rituals that led to warm memories, and of course favorite ice cream shops and candies that were available for a fraction of today's prices.

In addition, some people recognize a variety of unhealthy patterns of eating:

**WARNING**

✔ **Using food for comfort**

✔ **Eating out of boredom**

✔ **Overeating as rebellion**

✔ **Food-centered celebrations and rewards**

In order to take a healthy approach to feeding our children, we must first understand our own relationships with food and the early life experiences that shaped our eating habits and attitudes. It's helpful if we make a conscious effort to avoid repeating old patterns that may not be healthy, just familiar. Make thoughtful decisions about how to handle food and eating issues in your home. Think about the long-term benefits and negative consequences of the choices you're making and the messages that you are sending.

You may have some unhealthy eating habits and negative attitudes towards healthy foods to overcome, but you can do it. It's never too late to teach yourself and your children how to take better care of yourselves. This in itself is an important lesson to pass on to your children.

Get the kids involved in a family health makeover. Talk with them about the importance and the benefits of the following changes:

# Get More Active

**IDEA**

The television, video games, Internet, and telephone tend to make us all fall prey to living like couch potatoes. It may be a big change, but you can start with small steps:

✔ **Take a family walk after dinner**

✔ **Walk or bike to or home from school together instead of driving**

✔ **Take the furthest parking space instead of the closest one**

✔ **Take the stairs instead of the elevator**

✔ **Find a physical sport like tennis, swimming, hockey or soccer that the whole family can enjoy together. Play at least once a week (maybe just before your family meeting!)**

✔ **Plan a vacation that involves a fun physical activity like hiking,** biking, or skiing

✔ **Plan family fun days with the neighbors and do potato sack races, running relays, obstacle courses, and other fun events.**

✔ **Go on walking tours of surrounding towns.**

You can also sign the kids up for their own activities and find some adult activities that interest you. There are many different ways to get active... just get started. Like everything else, parental role modeling is important! If you spend much of your time with your feet up in the air, your credibility as a physical activity cheerleader will be shot! We were concerned about this, so at a family meeting we all agreed to join the YMCA and we work out and play together!

If your kids resist your efforts to increase the family exercise level, move forward without them and enjoy yourself. When they see how much fun you are having and how much more energetic you are feeling, they are sure to want to join in.

# Let's Eat Better

**MEAL TIME**

Here are some goals you can set for your family to improve your eating habits

✔ We'll limit fast food as much as possible. Eating fast food no more than once a month may be your goal, or it may be once a year. Decide what is possible for your family. Plan ahead so you are not in such a rush that you can't stop to get something healthy to eat. Sometimes this means planning your activities around meals at home or packing healthy meals and carrying a cooler. If you are in a pinch, be aware that some fast foods are better choices than others. You don't have to limit yourself to meals ordered through a speaker and passed through a window. A quick stop for a deli sandwich, for example, is usually more nutritious than a deep-fried anything! Even if it takes a minute or two longer, it's worth it.

✔ We'll fill our fridge and cupboards with more fruits, veggies, and healthy snacks and be much more selective about any chips, cookies, and treats that we bring home.

✔ We'll plan meals and cook together so that we have fun as we make our bodies healthier. We'll experiment with new varieties of foods and interesting recipes to make eating fun and adventuresome.

If you're really ambitious, think about planting a vegetable garden or a fruit tree in your backyard. Planting seeds, watering plants and eventually picking foods for dinner is exciting for children... and adults, too!

# How to Deal with Ordinary Challenges at the Table

> "One can say everything best over a meal."
> George Eliot (Mary Ann Evans)

**QUOTES**

When your child says, "I can't eat, I have at tummy ache," find out more about how badly their stomach is hurting. Once you have ruled out any major medical malfunction, let the child know that they need to rest and no snacks will be offered later. If they are feeling better they can have some plain toast or soup. It is better to err on the side of caution that to force an unwell child to eat. That said, keep track of any patterns that develop. If it seems that tummy aches always occur with meatloaf night, you'll need to find another way to address the issue. If the food aversion is that strong, plan an alternative option ahead of time. After all, if you really disliked sushi wouldn't you be upset if forced to eat it?

Many children are somewhat picky eaters. This is normal. It takes time to develop a taste for many different foods. Encourage variety, but accept that their range of acceptable foods will grow slowly. What you want to avoid is cooking ten different things to please the various taste preferences of your children. Let the children know that this is what we are having and if you don't prefer it you can have this one alternative or decide not to eat. Eventually, hunger sets in and they will learn to eat what is offered. But be reasonable… as adults we get to choose what we like and avoid what we don't for every meal. Don't reinforce picky eating by routinely offering your children's favorites as an alternative, but avoid regularly forcing your children to eat foods that make them miserable.

When your adolescent declares, "I'm a vegetarian," it can throw a real wrench into planning family meals. It is important to learn more about how this decision came about and what your child's goals are in being vegetarian. (I've never understood how we base so many children's stories on friendly cows and pigs and then expect that our kids will be happy to eat them...it was bound to rebound at some point!) Work together to investigate ways to be a healthy vegetarian – make sure that meat is replaced by other good sources of protein. Make sure your child understands that becoming a vegetarian requires a commitment to learning enough about vegetarian nutrition to stay healthy. However, if the reasons for being a vegetarian are not tied to any particular philosophy and simply reflect a fad among friends or an irrational fear of gaining weight, a heart to heart discussion needs to take place. Some young girls' vegetarianism reflects unhealthy attitudes about food and fear of fat and ought to be discouraged.

# Eating Disorders Awareness: Obesity

**QUOTES**

"Childhood obesity in America has greatly increased over the past few decades. It is estimated that 25-30% of children are overweight. Since the 1960s, obesity in children 6-11 years of age has increased 54% and there has been a 39% increase in adolescents 12-17 years of age."

Dr. Rebecca Moran, in *American Family Physician*

Many parents are concerned about making sure their children do not become overweight, especially if the parents have struggled with a weight problem themselves. There is good reason to be concerned.

Fast food, snacking, drinking high calorie beverages like soda and sweetened juices, advertisements that teach kids to ask their parents for junk food, and more television viewing and video games than ever are leading to fat kids! Lots of kids are surfing the net instead of riding their bikes and they mistakenly think that sugary cereals are part of a balanced breakfast. Skateboards are now motorized! Safety concerns lead to long carpool lines at schools and few students trekking home on foot. The cultural shifts in how our children spend their time have increased their energy intake (higher calories) and decreased their energy expenditure (less exercise).

Fortunately, these are the kinds of influences on obesity that we can battle. Teaching our children good eating behaviors and incorporating physical exercise as part of the family lifestyle are important factors in preventing childhood obesity. Following some of the tips discussed earlier will help you create a healthy eating environment for your entire family.

# Sometimes it is Genetic

Environment isn't the only thing that contributes to our children becoming overweight. Genetics seem to play a role as well. Children with obese parents are at greater risk of becoming obese themselves. Some of this risk factor may relate to the negative influence that the overweight parents may have on their children's eating behavior. Junk food junkies are more likely to raise junk food junkies!

**REMEMBER**

There is evidence that our genes influence our body shape and, at least to a certain extent, the amount of fat we have. Although we can't change our genes, we shouldn't passively accept that fatness runs in the family and assume there is nothing to avoid obesity. As will be discussed later, body acceptance is important. Short or tall, narrow or wide, "big boned" or "boney," it's helpful to embrace whatever our basic body shape is. Getting *dangerously* overweight, however, is something we can and should fight against.

It is generally accepted that severe obesity is associated with a variety of negative health consequences including hypertension and type-2 diabetes. Some people say that we are an anti-fat culture and the medical field is simply coming up with reasons to rationalize our negative views of obesity. There may be some truth in that, but there are enough studies to show relationships between obesity and illness to cause concern and work toward prevention.

In addition to concern for our children's physical health, we need to recognize the negative impact that being overweight has on our children's social and psychological well-being. We've discussed in Chapter 10 how any kid viewed as "different" is going to have difficulty gaining social acceptance among peers. Studies show that even very young children have negative stereotypes about overweight people and one study even showed that when given the choice of various playmates, a heavy child was least desired (kids were more likely to play with a handicapped child than one they perceived as fat).

The ugly truth is that we are judged on our appearance. These days, slimness is equated with beauty and people perceived as beautiful receive a whole host of social rewards like popularity in childhood and even higher salaries in adulthood. There is no doubt that heavier children often have a harder time in school. The increased likelihood of getting teased, left out, and being too embarrassed to participate in group sports are just not the ideal ingredients for a happy, healthy childhood.

The sooner you address the issue of your child being overweight, the better your outcome is likely to be. How should you handle it?

# Tips for Parents of Overweight Children

**IDEA**

✔ It is important to see the pediatrician to rule out any medical problems that may be triggering weight gain. Sometimes weight gain or weight loss signals that something aside from poor eating habits is going on.

✔ Never criticize, degrade, tease, or badger your child about his weight. The rest of the world will do plenty of that; your job is to help him develop and maintain high self-esteem at any weight or size. You may get frustrated at times, but remain supportive. If this is hard for you, imagine what it is like for him. Never tolerate teasing or any form of harassment from siblings. Teach them tolerance, patience, and compassion.

✔ As much as possible, avoid initiating a lot of talk about weight. Focus on concepts like being healthy and feeling great.

✔ Involve the whole family in making the kinds of changes that will help your child achieve optimum health. If the identified overweight child is given baked fish, plain rice, and no dessert for dinner when everyone else is eating pizza and ice cream, the child will feel resentful and bad about themselves. On the other hand, be sure not to deprive children without a weight problem because their sibling needs extra help. Make healthy choices that are good for *everyone*.

✔ Increase opportunities for physical activity and encourage the whole family to participate. If your overweight child is self-conscious about trying new activities, be understanding, patient, and reinforce him for trying. Find what he likes to do and *do it a lot*.

**199**

✔ Consult with a dietician/nutritionist who specializes in working with children. A specialist can teach the whole family about good nutrition as well as offer helpful hints to improve eating such as taking smaller bites, eating more slowly, and turning the television off when food is around. A good dietician may recommend some guidelines for fat, calories, etc., but generally speaking, strict dieting is not an effective long-term strategy for dealing with obesity. People lose weight on diets, but they can't keep it off. Instead they yo-yo for years. Don't get your child started on fad diets. In fact, avoid the word "diet" altogether...it sounds temporary and highly restrictive. Balanced, healthy and enjoyable eating for a lifetime is the goal.

✔ Seek counseling from a mental health professional with experience in treating childhood obesity. There are many behavior therapy techniques that are helpful to change lifestyle habits to promote healthy weight. Often times your child will not be the therapy client; the whole family will be in treatment together. That is usually the best approach, especially when more than one family member is overweight. A mental health counselor can be especially helpful when there are emotional, psychological issues related to the development of and the reaction to the weight problem.

In cases of very severe obesity, you may want to consider some of the special weight management programs designed for children that are available through some of the large universities. They have summer camps and a variety of services available. Without long-term consistency in following the program your child will return home only to regain the weight, so be sure you and your child are ready for a lifetime commitment to making healthy changes before enrolling.

A word of caution: There are no approved drugs to treat obesity in children, but clinical trials are underway. In addition, surgical procedures like gastric bypass are now being offered to adolescents. These are generally not options to consider except in very severe cases when serious medical conditions are present. Even in those cases, there are many potential side effects and complications that should not be taken lightly. If you find yourself this far down the road, get second, third, and fourth opinions from a variety of health professionals before proceeding.

**WARNING**

# Eating Disorders Awareness: Anorexia and Bulimia

Chances are you know someone, probably a teen-age girl or young woman, who suffers from anorexia or bulimia. Though the perception is that eating disorders are nearly impossible to treat, experts say that close to 90% of the time, people can overcome them.

Carol Sorgen, WebMD, in
*Overcoming Eating Disorders*

**QUOTES**

Be on the lookout for signs that your child may have an eating disorder. Anorexia nervosa is a disorder in which a diet escalates into obsessive food restriction, rapid weight loss, and fear of gaining weight.

**WARNING**

## Signs of Anorexia Nervosa

✔ Weight loss (15% below ideal weight)

✔ Wearing baggy clothing (to hide weight loss)

✔ Consistently making excuses for not eating and/or suddenly refusing to eat certain foods

✔ Adopting strange food rituals or rules about how certain foods are consumed

✔ Frequent weighing

✔ Complaints of feeling faint, fatigued, or frequently feeling cold in normal temperatures

✔ Hair loss

✔ Brittle nails

✔ Growth of a fine, fuzzy hair on the face and body

✔ Loss or interruption of the menstrual cycle

✔ Sneaking diet pills

✔ Negative body image

Often, individuals with anorexia are perfectionists and use their highly disciplined, obsessive style (that helps them earn good grades in school) to excel at weight loss. They are terrified of becoming fat and are usually in complete denial about their problem. People with anorexia often avoid social situations in which they may have to eat and they become isolated and withdrawn. Unfortunately, there are now pro-anorexia Web sites where one can easily learn new strategies to lose weight, hide the illness, and read bulletin boards filled with pro-thinness-at-any-cost messages. This is yet another reason to limit your kid's access to the Internet, as we talked about in Chapter Seven!

Another eating disorder is bulimia. This is a disorder in which an individual eats very large amounts of food in small periods of time (binges), and then purges the food or burns the calories (like vomiting, using laxatives, or over exercising). Some people with bulimia lose weight, but many others are of normal weight. Unlike anorexics, individuals with bulimia are more aware that their behavior is unhealthy and they may be more likely to discuss their problem or request help when it is offered.

**WARNING**

## Signs of Bulimia

✔ **Eating large amounts of food without gaining weight**

✔ **Sneaking food; large amounts of food disappearing from the house**

✔ **Frequent visits to the bathroom, especially right after a meal**

✔ **Tooth decay (due to the acid from vomiting)**

✔ **Puffy cheeks and/or red eyes**

✔ **Complaints of feeling faint or dizzy**

✔ **A strange odor (vomit) in the bathroom**

✔ **Hiding laxatives or diuretics**

✔ **Excessive exercise**

✔ **Negative body image**

Other signs of eating disorders include increased consumption of diet drinks and low- or non-fat foods. If your child is preoccupied with food, weight, and dieting and you suspect an eating disorder, discuss it

with them.  Be supportive and let them know that you are not angry
with them; you just want to understand what is going on.

Eating disorders are serious problems that require immediate attention.
*Seek professional help as soon as possible.*  Have your child examined by the
pediatrician to rule out medical conditions that may be contributing to
the food refusal and weight loss, and then to assess for any medical
complications resulting from an eating disorder.  You can contact the
International Association for Eating Disorder Professionals or use their
Web site at www.iaedp.com to find eating disorder specialists in your
area.  Treatment will often involve family therapy so that everyone will
understand more about what is going on and how to help make the
whole family healthier.

Although you have to be vigilant about your child's eating, one of the
biggest mistakes parents can make is having too much focus on or
exerting too much control over their children's eating.  Remember, *most*
children do not develop eating disorders.  Some children use food
refusal as a way of getting attention, and it almost always works.  It
may be negative attention, but it is attention nonetheless.  Try not to
overreact.  Don't turn your mealtimes into battles for control.

Early on, reinforce children for appropriate eating behaviors and
generally ignore the negative ones.  As discussed earlier, most children
end up eating what they need.  However, if your child's refusal to eat is
accompanied by some of the signs listed above, then investigate further
and take action.  Do not wait until your child is dangerously
underweight to see the doctor and take the steps needed for diagnosis
and treatment.

# When a Parent Has an Eating Disorder

Sometimes it is a parent who is struggling with an eating disorder.
Research shows that a parent's eating disorder can have a negative

impact on their children, so it is just as important that you seek treatment and do your best to manage and hopefully overcome your eating disorder. You owe this to yourself and to your family. As you seek treatment for yourself, do your best to avoid transferring your own unhealthy beliefs and attitudes about food and weight to your children. Be aware of any unrealistic concerns you may have about their eating or weight, and don't act upon them. We know one mother whose obsession with weight included her children. They were raised on skim milk and nonfat foods and, not surprisingly, one child is now an overweight young adult who is likely struggling with body image and eating issues of his own.

# Promoting Healthy Body Image at Home

**TOGETHER**

There has always been pressure on teenagers to look a certain way. Teens have always been slaves to trends in clothing, hairstyles and make-up. Looking like you fit in or are obviously trying to stick out from the crowd is a big part of adolescence. But these days, trying to look like their favorite pop idol has gotten increasingly difficult, if not impossible, for kids. But body image disturbance is not just an issue for teens: surveys have shown that girls as young as six are dissatisfied with their bodies, and the research consistently shows that about 40% of elementary school girls and 25% of elementary school boys are dissatisfied with their weight and want to be thinner, even when they are not overweight!

For girls, trying to be like the sometimes surgically altered physiques of their favorite pop stars and fashion models is not only hard, it can be deadly. There are unrealistic representations of beauty and thinness in every form of media imaginable. As a result, a rising number of girls are unhappy with their bodies and are starting diets younger and younger. For some girls, dieting becomes an obsession and their efforts to get thin get out of control and lead to anorexia nervosa. For others, failed attempts to restrict food intake result in the chronic binge-purge pattern of bulimia nervosa. Most girls do not develop full-blown eating disorders, but many of them struggle with decreased self-esteem, depression, and anxiety because of the gap between how they want to look and how they see themselves. In addition, the rapid physical changes of adolescence often are hard to accept since increased body fat and hips are not exactly all the rage these days.

For boys, pro wrestlers and larger than life action heroes serve as ideals that are nearly impossible to emulate, especially for younger boys. Pressures to look and be athletic increase as boys become more involved with sports. Some boys want to lose weight to look better, while others think they are too thin. To bulk up, an increasing number of young males are turning to unhealthy strategies like using anabolic steroids. Although illegal to use, access is frighteningly easy through the Internet and workout gyms. The side effects can be troublesome: hair loss, acne, and testicular shrinkage among other things. You would think these negative effects would be deterrent enough, but the fact that young males will tolerate them to reach their physical strength and appearance goals tells us just how important these things can become to them.

# Parental Influences: Role Modeling and Feedback

**REMEMBER**

Without realizing it, we send messages about the importance of appearance on a daily basis through our own behavior:

"Do I look fat in this?" When you ask your family members for this type of feedback, you are communicating that you are worried about your weight and that it is important to avoid looking fat... fat is bad. "Am I losing my hair?" or "Do you think I need a facelift?" have similar effects in sending the message that you are unhappy and concerned about your appearance. We should aim to teach our children a healthy level of concern that motivates them to stay well groomed and appropriately dressed, not a concern that will lead to chronic dissatisfaction with physical appearance. So, be careful what you say in the dressing room or in front of the mirror at home. Your children are observing your self-critical words and actions and will take their cues from you when it comes to attitudes about looks.

Dieting is another way that teaches our children that we have to get or stay thin. Although the motivation to lose weight probably includes desiring improved health, that's not what the kids see and hear. They hear about how you have to fit back into this or that outfit, how a wedding or reunion is coming up and you need to look good, or how summer is on the way and you are dreading swimsuit season. When you start to lose weight, they probably witness the compliments about how great you look and see that you are focused on your improved appearance. So, rather than go on a diet, focus on some of the tips described earlier in the chapter and work toward a *healthy lifestyle* for the whole family.

Demonstrate self-acceptance, self-confidence, and a positive attitude about appearance. This doesn't mean you need to act arrogant or feign high levels of appearance satisfaction, it just means that you show your children you are comfortable in your own skin. Replacing self-deprecating remarks and insecure behaviors with a focus on feeling good, gracefully accepting compliments, and occasionally acknowledging that you are pleased with some aspect of your appearance can be helpful.

It goes without saying that the lessons of "you can't judge a book by its cover" and "it's what's on the inside that counts" will go a long way to teach your children the values that will help them temper our cultural emphasis on physical appearance. Reinforce that personality counts... there is even research to prove it. A recent study by Dr. Stacey Tantleff-Dunn and her graduate student Brian Fisak showed that when a person is described as having many positive personality characteristics such as being friendly and kind, people are more generous in evaluating that individual's attractiveness.

In addition, how we feel about ourselves can impact how people perceive us. So if we teach our children not to focus too much on physical appearance in evaluating themselves or others, to hold their heads up high and know that they are terrific just the way they are (as Mr. Rogers has always suggested), and embrace the ways that make them unique and special, others are more likely to pick up on their confidence and see them as the beautiful creatures they are. If they don't, it is their own problem.

Not only do we have to be careful about how we deal with our own appearance, but heightened sensitivity to how we respond to our children's appearance is equally if not more important. Dr. Stacey's research has shown that feedback on physical appearance comes in many forms, sometimes as very subtle gestures or facial expressions, and other times it is expressed with direct comments.

Negative feedback on appearance can be very damaging to one's body image and self-esteem, so be very thoughtful about how you respond to your children's physical appearance. Teasing about looks is commonplace, not just at school but frequently at home. Research shows that brothers are often the worst about teasing their siblings, but parents may join in as well. At first teasing and joking seem playful and the intent may be to help a child develop a sense of humor about a physical characteristic that is unusual in some way. However, more often than not this approach helps the child to create long-lasting insecurities.

Teasing is one of the strongest predictors of body dissatisfaction. Although they may seem to be laughing right along with you, children who are teased may experience a great deal of emotional pain and self-consciousness that persists through adulthood. People don't typically forget their nicknames like "Dumbo" (for big ears) "chicken legs" or "hippo hips" even if they have changed a great deal physically. So, ban teasing about appearance in your house. When a child brings up his or her own concerns about their appearance that is the time to compassionately discuss the issue and possibly infuse some humor into their thinking about it without ever making fun of them. In addition, be sure that the majority of compliments exchanged in your home are non-appearance related.

Compliment them on their maturity, intelligence, and their caring nature. Those qualities, unlike looks, are much more important and everlasting.

Children develop their self-concept through the eyes of their parents and loved ones. We take that influence very seriously. Remember that even disapproving facial expressions and not offering dessert with the qualifier, "you're getting a little chubby" can be hurtful. Yes, of course, you want your kids to look good and feel good about themselves. Feedback is an important part of helping them learn how to dress well and take good care of themselves. Just be sure to offer your advice in a very constructive, positive, affirming way. "Ya know, I think you would look great with a haircut that allowed us to see your eyes again" is a whole lot more constructive than "You look silly with that long hair – get it cut!"

In the same vein, it's important to allow your kids to experiment with their looks. Try not to freak out when your toddler puts and outfit of a polka dotted shirt with striped pants or colors that clash... focus on the fact that they are taking the initiative to dress themselves. Only for important events like formal gatherings should you intervene. If your teenager wants purple hair, talk about why you are concerned about it, but then just be thankful that hair color is temporary. Save the arguing for when they request a piercing or tattoo!

# Out of the Mouths of Babes

"Mommy, why does that woman have a mustache?" asked the Dunns' daughter, Nickie, when she was three. Embarrassing for them for sure, but not as bad as when she wondered aloud, "What's that big hanging moley thing on that lady's face" when she was two, or when she exclaimed while holding her nose, "Yuck, that man smells pewey!" We have all been there! Children learn about the world and the people in it by asking questions. When something looks or smells different about someone they'll notice, and in Nickie's case, comment loudly about it. How you handle these golden opportunities to teach your children about physical appearance is critical.

Explain that everybody is different and that is what makes the world so great. How boring it would be if we all looked exactly the same. Then, explain what is different about the person. Stacey said something along the lines of: "Well, I know you are used to seeing mustaches on men, but sometimes women can have facial hair, too. Some women may choose to remove it, and other women are perfectly fine with having it. It's just another difference that makes life more interesting." An important piece of advice Stacey shared after the "mole incident" was, "I know you have lots of questions about people we see when we are out. It may be best if you wait to ask me those questions when we're alone so that we're sure not to hurt anybody's feelings. Some people don't really like when we comment about what they look like or what they are doing." That seemed to do the trick. At four, Nickie still has many questions, but she has learned to ask them at more appropriate times in a more curious and less disgusted manner.

Feedback is a two-way street. We talked about the need for you to be cautious about the feedback you give your kids, but you don't have control over what your young children have in store for you. The innocence and honesty of kids is usually so endearing, but it can be a bit difficult to cope with at times. Their honest critiques of and questions about your physical characteristics can make for some interesting moments.

When your children ask you a question or offer their opinion in a way that seems like blatant criticism ("Why does your tummy hang down over your panties?" was a question I overheard some poor woman receive in a dressing room, and my son once announced that he loved playing with my flab under my arms!), try not to react negatively.

Children rarely mean to hurt your feelings. As hard as it may be, especially when they pick on your weaknesses, you need to react calmly and think of yourself as a teacher. I tend to handle embarrassing situations with humor, but I also mention how their comments could hurt someone's feelings. In these situations, I tell my child that I know you didn't intend to be hurtful, but we should be really careful about pointing out differences in people's physical appearance. In a situation like this, a good response might be something like, "My tummy looks different because I have had babies. My tummy had to stretch so much when the babies grew and it never quite went back to the way it was. But that's okay, I still love my tummy and I still look great." Asking to see the little girl's tummy and a giving it a little tickle would be a great way to move on.

# Exercises for Food, Eating, and Body Image Issues

## "Taking Inventory of Your Views on Food"

> Big Hint #1: This is a great opportunity to learn about the foods you keep in your house and possibly even clean up and organize.

**REMEMBER**

**Step 1:** Start with the refrigerator. For each item you find, write down exactly what it is and then write what kind of food it is. An example would be: soda, non-nutritional beverage; eggs, protein; cake, dessert food; etc. After you throw away any spoiled foods take away as much clutter and add as much organization as you can to your refrigerated items. Are the fruits and veggies easily accessible? Are they washed and cut up, ready for consumption? What is hidden behind the tall bottles? Are there some healthy foods hiding out of reach?

**Step 2:** Next hit the freezer. Even frozen items don't last forever, so get rid of any really old frostbitten foods that nobody will ever eat. Then, inventory what you've got.

**Step 3:** Proceed to the pantry and the cupboards. Many more non-nutritional foods are likely to be lurking there, so be sure to write down all of the chips, the candies, and other snacks and treats that you have accumulated. Once again, toss any items that are past their prime (stale, moldy, etc.!). Think organization as you put things back. Consider placing all of your candy (if you have any) in a special treat box and keep other snacks in a special snack section.

**Step 4:** Now it's time to review your inventory. Tally up the nutritious foods and then look at the total number of foods that don't offer much nourishment. How is the balance? The goal is not to get rid of all snack and dessert foods. For many families that is neither realistic nor desirable. Striking a healthy balance is what is important!

Avoid labeling foods as "good" or "bad." Foods are not inherently good or bad, it's how we eat them that determine whether they are okay or not. Focus on noting which foods you should eat more sparingly and those that are great for staying healthy. Based on your inventory, decide which foods ought to be available in greater quantities or with easier access, and which foods you could probably do without.

## "Taste Test Challenge"

**Step 1:** This is a game of trust and culinary adventure. First, agree that nobody will feed anybody else anything that is not edible, or intentionally "disgusting."

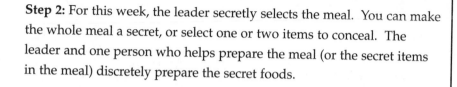

> **Big Hint #1:** The goal of the exercise is to trust each other as you try new foods or have fun identifying foods you have always enjoyed.

**IDEA**

**Step 2:** For this week, the leader secretly selects the meal. You can make the whole meal a secret, or select one or two items to conceal. The leader and one person who helps prepare the meal (or the secret items in the meal) discretely prepare the secret foods.

**Step 2:** During the meal, everyone else wears blindfolds. (Bandanas from the dollar store make great blindfolds if you don't have anything handy at home.)

**Step 3:** Each blindfolded family member takes at least one taste of the secret food(s). They can touch the food if they'd like.

**Step 4:** They discuss what they think they taste and what they think about the taste. Blindfolds are then removed and the foods are revealed.

**Step 5:** Discuss how the blindfold affected your perceptions of the food. Were there any surprises?

**REMEMBER**

**IDEA**

## "Mirror, Mirror Off the Wall"

> **Big Hint #1: This is a family challenge to help you gain insight into what importance each of you places on how you look, and how you rely on others to let you know if your appearance is acceptable.**

**Step 1:** Pick a day when everyone will be home for at least a large portion of the day. Cover every mirror in the house. You can use newspaper, butcher paper, garbage bags… anything that will completely hide all reflections. The rule for the day is that nobody can look into any mirror, anywhere, at any time. Anyone who leaves the house agrees not to look in a mirror while out. To take this a step further, you can decide as a family if any cosmetics or hair styling will be allowed for the day. Taking those things away may make this an even more effective learning opportunity.

> **Big Hint #2: Do this on a holiday, or a day that nobody has to go to work or school.**

**Step 2:** As the day progresses, discuss how you feel about not seeing yourself. You can ask each for help as needed. What does it feel like to rely on each other for feedback on your hair, etc.? How did not seeing yourself affect your day, if at all? Was it harder for some family members than others? If so, what made it harder or easier for each of you?

**Step 3:** Discuss how to have a balanced view of physical appearance in your home. How much concern about looks is too much? Not enough? Do you each have realistic views of your beauty? Do you agree upon how important outer vs. inner beauty is?

# What Have We Learned?

I know there was a lot to digest in this chapter (okay, bad joke) but it is important to realize that our best efforts at getting our kids to eat well and look nice can sometimes rebound on us. You've learned some tips on how to look for danger signs that you or your kids may be leaning towards eating disorders, and you've got some tools with which to combat eating disorders if they do crop up in your family.

# Chapter Twelve

# Chapter Thirteen
## Drug Issues

## Why Do People Take Drugs?

"For parents who believe they have little influence over their children, teens tell us their parents do influence them in resisting drugs while friends are the main influence for those teens who decide to use drugs. More teens who don't use marijuana (42%) credit their parents over any other influence."
National Center on Addiction and
Substance Abuse at Columbia University (CASA)

**QUOTES**

Drugs. It's the big bugaboo – the one single topic that scares parents all over the country, regardless of where they live. It's always lurking somewhere in the back of your mind, the fact that sooner or later somebody is going to offer your kids drugs, and you're not going to be there to help them make the proper choices. Well, you won't be there, but you can let your kids know in no uncertain terms how you feel about drugs and you might be pleasantly surprised at the results garnered from all that time put in around the family table talking about topics just like this.

When your kids are younger, it's easier to tell them to stay away from drugs using simplistic terms and reasoning. When they ask you why people take drugs, you can just tell them:

✔ **Because they think it's cool:**
Some people take drugs because they want to be seen as cool, or they're scared that if they don't take drugs they'll be seen as a loser or a nerd. So they make bad decisions, like taking drugs, to cover-up their insecurities. But those who decide to take drugs are the ones who are most likely to be unhappy and unsuccessful in life.

✔ **Because they can't deal with reality:**
When kids take drugs they're just admitting they're not confident enough to deal with their problems or brave enough to reach out for help. So they just get high and forget about it. But their problems just get worse when they take drugs!

✔ **Because they're bored:**
Lots of people turn to drugs for a little excitement. But people who make these kinds of decisions usually find out that drugs are ultimately unfulfilling and painful. In general, the only people who take drugs because they're bored are really boring people in the first place.

✔ **Because the media says it's cool:**
All sorts of movies and TV shows picture people getting drunk and high, and having a great time. But those sorts of movies and TV shows never show what happens the next day, or the next year, when all the bad effects of taking drugs and alcohol set in.

✔ **Because they think it makes them seem grown-up:**
The reality is, the most grown-up people out there aren't drug users. The real grown-ups are confident, smart, aware, and compassionate, unlike drug users, who are insecure, clueless, and selfish.

Those sorts of answers will work when the kids are really young. But as your kids approach middle school age, you'll have to get a little bit more sophisticated in your answers. You really need to start talking to your kids seriously about drugs before they hit middle school, because that's where somebody will probably offer them drugs for the first time. It is an ongoing discussion at our dinner table.

# Middle School Kids and Gateway Drugs

Many adolescents say they began experimenting with substances when they were children. Unfortunately, we don't have much information on the extent of drug abuse among children. But surveys of youth tell a frightening story. For example, according to a Federal Government 1997 *Monitoring the Future* study, by the time they reached the eighth grade:

**Alcohol:** More than 54% of the children surveyed had tried alcohol.

**Tobacco:** 47% had tried cigarettes
.

**Marijuana:** 23% of eighth graders had smoked marijuana at least once and 10% had smoked it within the past 30 days – up from 3% 1991. Also, kids find it's easy to get and think it's safe to use.

Inhalants: 21% experimented with inhalants – inexpensive and easily found in household products such as glue, aerosols, and solvents, these dangerous substances are most often abused in early adolescence.

> The National Youth Anti-Drug Media
> Campaign's Behavior Change Expert Panel

**WARNING**

Some of you might be surprised to see alcohol and tobacco mentioned when we're discussing drugs, but the latest thinking is that these are among the most dangerous because they're now considered "gateway drugs." Gateway drugs are substances that people take which, in many cases, lead to those people taking more and harder drugs. It's as if by doing one thing, the kids have broken a barrier, so it becomes easier for them to break the next rule down the line. Alcohol and tobacco are particularly sneaky gateway drugs due to the plain fact that they're legal and easily available in far too many places.

And kids aren't even aware that alcohol and tobacco are drugs. According to the Substance Abuse and Mental Health Services Administration, 2.6 million young people do not know that a person can die of an overdose of alcohol. We have a friend who works in the hospital ER. We had her spend an evening with our pre-teen and teenage daughters telling the horrible scenarios she sees in the ER from teenagers using alcohol. Some of her stories involved drinking and driving but most of them regarded overdoses of alcohol. We feel it did the trick.

We should all know by now that cigarettes are just a slow boat to lung disease and cancer, but how many of us know that cigarette smoking triggers the release of dopamine into the brain? And how many of us know that when a person takes a hit of crack cocaine – or a drag on a cigarette – the drugs cause a spike in dopamine levels in the brain, and a rush of euphoria, or pleasure. It's the same thing, only on a different level. While it's not the only chemical involved in drug abuse, experts have come to believe that dopamine is the crucial one.

These are the sorts of hard facts you need to lay out on the family table when you're talking to your middle school kids about drugs.

It's unfortunate that our society provides drug information to children in ways that are just not effective in reducing kids' use of drugs. For example, despite the fact that children know more about the adverse consequences of cigarette smoking than ever before, use of cigarettes among teenagers is unaffected. We have spent a great deal of time and money educating children about the long-term consequences of alcohol and drug use.

Unfortunately, children tend to operate on short term gain rather than being concerned about the distant future. This is why teenagers continue to smoke. They are completely unconcerned abut dying from lung disease in 30 or more years. When talking to kids about drugs, it is critical to focus on short-term negative consequences that they care about. For example, in many states, an underage alcohol use violation can prevent teenagers from getting a driver's license for several years. This is an extremely powerful motivator to keep kids from underage drinking.

Another helpful approach is to help kids understand the harm to their families and others they can cause with drug use behavior. Letting them know how much they are cared for by you and others and how devastated all of you would be if something bad happened to them is very important. This is vital a message that can easily be lost when we lose communication with teens.

Finally, making sure your kids are aware of negative consequences experienced by kids very similar to them is another way to make an impact. Highlight news stories of kids their age in their town who are caught in drug busts, underage alcohol use, driving under the influence, etc.

# It's Not the Same Old Pot Anymore

**QUOTES**

> 140,000 people are admitted to US hospitals every year because of marijuana abuse, mainly with mental health problems. That's one in every 140 marijuana users.
>
> Dr Patrick Dixon, in *The Truth about Marijuana*

Admit it, you either smoked some pot when you were growing up, or you knew some kids who did, and you all turned out okay. That might still be the case today, if it wasn't for the fact that pot isn't the same drug that it was in the 1960s and 1970s. Some parents who saw marijuana being widely used in their youth still wonder, "Is marijuana really so bad for my child?" We think it is!

**REMEMBER**

> "The potency of marijuana today is greater than it was in the 1970s, and increased potency means increased addiction potential. The implications for a teen's growing body are long-term and dangerous."
>
> Ariel White-Kovach, executive director,
> Hazelden Center for Youth & Families

We need to be telling our kids that beyond the clear fact that marijuana is a gateway drug – nobody ever woke up one morning and stuck a needle in their arm, they all started out by smoking pot – it's now a heavyweight drug all on its own. The people who grow pot have gotten better at it over the years, and some estimates state that the potency of the pot kids are smoking now is twenty to thirty times stronger than the pot people smoked in the 1970s.

Perhaps most importantly, very recent scientific evidence has clearly linked marijuana use to lung disease and early death. The level of carcinogens in marijuana is approximately 10 times more than tobacco.

We need to tell our kids very clearly that we will be very disappointed if they tried using marijuana. Tell them that marijuana use interferes with kid's concentration, memory, and motor skills, and that it interferes with motivation, leads to poorer school performance, and can cause users to disappoint the people most important to them.

And you already know that this doesn't have to be a lecture. You can state this all clearly during a family meal or meeting and end up by saying, "I love you and I want the best for you, so I hope you won't try marijuana."

# What We Need to Tell Our Kids About Pot

✔ Marijuana is illegal.

✔ Marijuana now exists in forms that are stronger – with higher levels of THC, the psychoactive ingredient – than in the 1960s.

**WARNING**

✔ Studies show that someone who smokes five joints a week may be taking in as many cancer-causing chemicals as someone who smokes a full pack of cigarettes every day.

✔ Hanging around users of marijuana often means being exposed not only to other illegal drugs, but also to a lifestyle that can include trouble in school, engaging in sexual activity while young, unintended pregnancy, difficulties with the law, and other problems.

✔ Marijuana use can slow down reaction time and distort

✔ perceptions. This can interfere with athletic performance, decrease a sense of danger, and increase risk of injury.

✔ Regular marijuana users can lose the ability to concentrate that is needed to master important academic skills, and they can experience short-term memory loss. Habitual marijuana users tend to do worse in school and are more likely to drop out altogether.

✔ Teens that rely on marijuana as a chemical crutch and refuse to face the challenges of growing up never learn the emotional, psychological, and social lessons of adolescence.

The research is not complete on the effects of marijuana on the developing brain and body.

> The National Youth Anti-Drug Media
> Campaign's Behavior Change Expert Panel

You need to be talking with your kids in an open and honest manner about how the seemingly harmless gateway drugs like alcohol, tobacco and marijuana not only can lead to harder drugs, but they are dangerous in and of themselves. These conversations need to be held early and often!

Here are some tips for general substance abuse type conversations:

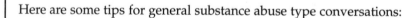

✔ **Be absolutely clear with your kids that you don't want them using drugs.** Ever. Anywhere. Don't leave room for interpretation. And talk often about the dangers and results of drug and alcohol abuse. Once or twice a year won't do it. Keep in mind the fact that whether you see it or not, in most cases, your kids see drug use among their peers daily.

**EXAMPLE**

✔ **Be a better listener.** Ask questions – and encourage them.

Paraphrase what your child says to you. Ask for their input about family decisions. Showing your willingness to listen will make your child feel more comfortable about opening up to you.

✔ **Give honest answers.** Don't make up what you don't know; offer to find out. If asked whether you've ever taken drugs, let them know what's important: that you don't want them using drugs. This can be a tough topic and refusing to give them a straight answer to a straight question can affect your relationship. If you admit to your kids that you experimented with drugs, also admit that it was a big mistake, and now that you know more about drugs, you are very thankful that you survived it.

✔ **Use TV reports, anti-drug commercials, or school discussions** about drugs to help you introduce the subject in a natural, unforced way.

✔ **Don't react in a way that will cut off further discussion.** If your child makes statements that challenge or shock you, turn them into a calm discussion of why your child thinks people use drugs, or whether the effect is worth the risk.

✔ **Role-play with your child and practice ways to refuse drugs in different situations.** Acknowledge how tough these moments can be and use this as an opportunity to reinforce the idea that staying away from kids who use drugs will prevent your kids from having to refuse them. And there are lots or reasons to avoid those kids. Your kids need to know that they can be found guilty of crimes simply by being associated with other kids who use drugs We share with our kids that the chances of a "friend" offering you drugs is more probable than the stereotypical kid they think of. This is when being confident in 'who they are" and being able to say NO is important.

The more often you start to communicate on these problems, the more at ease your child will feel about discussing drugs and other sensitive issues with you. Try and remember to use the methods we discussed and the assertive style of communication we talked about in Chapter Six.

# But I See You Drinking Mom...

When your child sees you enjoying a beer at a family barbecue, or having a cocktail at a party, you can be sure that somewhere down the road when you're having a discussion about the dangers of drugs, they will throw the question of your alcohol or tobacco use into play. And as long as you're striving as hard as you can to be a good role model, as we discussed in Chapter Seven, this shouldn't be too hard to handle.

You can simply tell your child that you understand the dangers of abuse, but as an adult you choose to use alcohol with caution. Explain that when a person becomes of legal drinking age they can decide whether or not they will choose to drink in moderation. If your child points out that you're often drunk and you don't exhibit moderation, then you need to seriously think about your alcohol use and the negative effect it is having on your family and yourself.

And as far as smoking goes... come on! It's indefensible! You just have to acknowledge to your child that you began smoking when you were too young to know better, and now you're addicted. Explain that someday, when you're ready, you'll try to quit and you'll expect your kids' full support when you do. At this point you can explain to your kids that you never want them to have to face this problem for themselves, so they should never start smoking.

And then you should quit smoking. Really! You already know it's a bad habit, and not one you wish to exhibit as a role model. And worst of all, the data on smoking clearly indicate that if you don't quit smoking, it will kill you, one way or another, no doubt about it.

# Did You Ever Smoke Pot?

Be prepared to answer the big question your kids are bound to ask someday, "Did you ever use drugs?" And if you never did, good for you – you can look them right in the eye and say you didn't, and tell them why you stayed away from drugs.

You should also arm yourself with up to date information on drugs to be prepared to see potential threats to your kids. One good example is the drug MDMA, often called "Ecstasy." MDMA has been used by thousands of teenagers at dance parties called "raves." If questioned by their parents, many of these kids probably told them they were just going to a dance party for innocent fun. However, it is common knowledge that many of these parties are completely organized around selling party-goers MDMA. Even worse, evidence is mounting that even small amounts of MDMA use can cause significant brain damage that users are not aware of until years later. As a parent, you must know what the threats to your kids are and how to recognize them.

When your kids ask if you did drugs, and you did use drugs, then you have a very tough choice to make. One option is to lie about your history. Every family's situation is different and there may be situations in which it would be best to keep the truth from your family. Only you can make that decision.

However, it is possible to honestly tell your kids that you "experimented' with drugs when you were growing up or in college (still growing up!) *and* that it was a very bad decision. You can tell them that you are thankful that you survived the experience, but you will do anything you can to keep your kids from taking chances with their health and their entire future. By admitting to your kids that you made mistakes as a kid, it can open the lines of communication and strengthen your relationship.

It is critical, however, to make sure that your kids know that you really believe your behavior was a mistake, you regret it (you're even embarrassed about it!), and that the only reason you are telling them about it is that you value your relationship too much to lie to them. It is also helpful to tell them that one of the main jobs of being a parent is to make sure your kids avoid the mistakes that you made and you will do everything you can to make sure they avoid the mistake of using drugs.

There are many other things you can add to this conversation including the fact that we know much more today about the dangers of using drugs. Nicotine has been found to be as addictive as crack cocaine, but cigarette smoking used to be completely accepted and even encouraged in our culture. But as we have learned more and more about the addiction potential of nicotine and the death sentence that tobacco imposes on users, we have gradually moved toward making tobacco use completely illegal. And drugs that are currently illegal are illegal for good reasons. There are numerous resources to help you find up to date and scientifically accurate information to help your kids understand the nature of the dangers posed by drugs.

However, beware of Web sites or other sources that are unreliable. Your kids may even search the internet to find information that would appear to make drug use look harmless. This kind of information is not correct but continues to be spread by people who are not experts. You can take it from one of our co-authors who is a drug scientist and clinical psychologist, all drugs are harmful, absolutely no doubt about it. The best resources for specific information are the Web sites of the National Institute on Drug Abuse (www.nida.gov) and the National Institute on Alcohol Abuse and Alcoholism (www.niaaa.gov).

So, if you did use drugs and you feel that you can be honest about your history – or if you used drugs so extensively that it is common knowledge – here are some possible responses to the dreaded "Did you ever use drugs?" question:

**IDEA**

✔ "I took drugs because some of my friends used them, and I thought I needed to in order to fit in. In those days, people didn't know as much as they do now about all the bad things that can happen when you smoke marijuana or do other drugs. If I'd known then what I know now, I never would have tried them, and I'll do everything I can to keep you away from drugs."

✔ "Everyone makes mistakes, and when I used drugs, I made a big one. I'm telling you about this, even though it's embarrassing, because I love you, and I want to save you from making the same stupid decision that I made when I was your age. You can learn from my mistakes without repeating them."

✔ "I did drugs because I was bored and wanted to take some risks, but I soon found that I couldn't control the risks – they were controlling me. There are much better ways of challenging yourself than doing drugs."

✔ "At your age, between homework, friends, sports, and other interests, there are a lot of fun things going on. If you get into taking drugs, you're pretty much giving up those other things, because you may stop being able to concentrate, control your moods or keep to a schedule. You'll miss out on all these great experiences, and you'll never get those times back."

✔ "You don't know how your body will react to drugs. Some people can get addicted really quickly or can get really sick or even die using a drug for the first time."

✔ "I started doing drugs when I was young, and I've been battling them ever since. They made me miss a big part of growing up, and every day I have to stay positive so they don't make me miss more – my job, my relationships, and my time with you. I love you too much to watch you fight a similar battle."

The National Youth Anti-Drug Media
Campaign's Behavior Change Expert Panel

You need to reinforce the fact that you know you made a mistake, and that the past is the past. You also need to let them know that whatever you did has no relevance to what is happening now, and they have clear rules that they need to follow.

# Making Rules About Drug Use

QUOTES

"Children tell us that their parents can be the single greatest influence in their decisions not to smoke or use alcohol or drugs. Recent surveys by CASA show that, for many children, parents are the single biggest determinant in these decisions – stronger than that of friends, teachers and media. In short, the impact of parents is more important than commonly thought. Your power as a parent comes from several sources, and its effectiveness is marked by the time spent with your children and the consistency of the messages you give them."

CASA

Your kids need to know explicitly, in no unclear terms, that when it comes to drugs and alcohol there will be a clear and non-negotiable punishment. Research shows that kids are less likely to use tobacco, alcohol, and other drugs if their parents set clear rules about not doing so.

## Here are some rulemaking tips:

Set clear rules – and discuss in advance the consequences of breaking them. Don't make empty threats or let the rule-breaker off the hook. Don't impose harsh or unexpected new punishments.

**REMEMBER**

✔ **The rules must be consistently enforced;** every time a child breaks the rules the parent should enforce a "punishment."

✔ **"Punishments" should involve appropriate consequences that fit the offense.** Overly severe punishments serve to undermine the quality of the parent-child relationship.

✔ **Set a curfew.** And enforce it strictly. Be prepared to negotiate for special occasions.

✔ **Have kids check in at regular times when they're away from home or school.** Give them a phone card, change or even a pager with clear rules for using it. ("When I beep you, I expect a call back within 15 minutes.")

✔ **Call parents whose home is to be used for a party.** On party night, don't be afraid to stop in to say hello (and make sure that adult supervision is in place). I have dropped by with some pizza and ice cream at one of my daughters parties. When I came in I said, "I happened to be in the neighborhood, and I was thinking of you guys, but I can't stay." I think my message was clear – I just wanted them to know that I may be doing that at anytime!

✔ **Make it easy to leave a party where drugs are being used.** Discuss in advance how to signal you or another designated adult who will come to pick your child up the moment he or she feels uncomfortable. Later, be prepared to talk about what happened.

✔ **Listen to your instincts.** Don't be afraid to intervene if your gut reaction tells you that something is wrong.

adapted from *Parents, The Anti-Drug*

# If You Think Your Kid May be Using Drugs

Neal and I wanted to understand what was going on "out there," and what was available to help parents who were worried about substance abuse. One wonderful resource was our county's drug program. (Drug Free Community in Orange County) They had a video for parents to show the current drugs, slang names and the effects. Check to see if such a video is available form your local government.

**WARNING**

Three types of risk factors increase the chances that children will turn to alcohol, tobacco, and illegal drugs:

**Child risk factors,** such as serious behavior problems, attention-deficit hyperactivity disorder (ADHD), violent acting out, alienation, or rebelliousness.

**Family risk factors,** such as communication difficulties, too much or too little discipline, parents' use of substances, and child abuse or neglect.

**Environmental risk factors,** such as peer rejection, lax enforcement of purchase-by-minors laws, extreme poverty, neighborhood crime, and failure to do well in school.

*Parents, The Anti-Drug*

If, despite all your hard work and communication efforts, you still think there may be a chance that your kids are using drugs, you need to take some immediate action. There are no easy answers here! Don't ignore the signs. If you just see one or two of the signs below, it could be that your child is going through puberty or adolescence and is getting a little weird. That happens. But if you see more than three or four of these signs, then you need to take action. Early intervention can stave off a lifetime of sorrow!

Here are some things to watch for if you think your child may be drinking or using drugs:

**WARNING**

✔ Low grades or poor school performance

✔ Withdrawal, isolation, depression or fatigue

✔ Aggressive rebellious behavior

✔ Truancy

✔ Excessive influence by peers or change in friends

✔ Hostility and lack of cooperativeness

✔ Deteriorating relationships with family

✔ Loss of interest in appearance and personal hygiene

✔ Loss of interest in hobbies and sports

✔ Changes in sleeping and eating habits

✔ Evidence of drugs and paraphernalia

✔ Physical changes such as: red eyes, runny nose, frequent sore throats, rapid weight loss, bruises from falls

CASA, *Parent Power*

# What To Do if You See the Signs of Drug Use

Talk to your child immediately. If you feel you need help with this, contact your doctor, a school social worker or clergy member, your local hospital, the county medical health society or a family counselor. Professional help may be necessary, depending on the level of substance abuse. Keep in mind that the moment that you find out about this activity is not solely the moment that you need to impose punishment. While you should definitely make your kids pay the clear consequences we talked about above, you should also try and re-open communication lines and bond together to solve the problem.

Here's something to keep in mind: As with most critical communication decisions facing your child, it is important to remember that overreaction is the wrong reaction. Keep calm if you discover your child is using drugs. Don't be afraid to seek professional help.

# What Have We Learned?

After reading this chapter, you should better understand some of the ways that you can help your kids steer clear of drug use and abuse. You've got some tips and tools to help guide your kids into following a path that will help them avoid some of the many problems legal and illegal drug use can bring. You should also be thinking about how you as a parent can exhibit better role model qualities if you use alcohol and tobacco immoderately. By completing the exercises you just read about you'll have an easily accomplished, simple and structured way to talk to your kids about drugs and substance abuse issues.

# Chapter Fourteen
## Family Stress Issues

## Dealing With Stress as a Family

"The healthy way to deal with stress or to work through feelings of loss or sadness is to talk about it with someone – a family member, a close friend, a pastor, or a professional counselor. Many persons who experience stress or loss deny or ignore the normal feelings of anger, guilt, fear, and sorrow which accompany these experiences. Such denial can lead to emotional or physical difficulties. At a minimum, it is likely to lead to a breakdown in communication with others, thus blocking the natural means of recovering from the stress, grief, or change"

> Ronald L. Pitzer, Family Sociologist, School
> of Social Work, College of Human Ecology,
> University of Minnesota

**QUOTES**

We've all got a certain amount of stress in our lives and we've all got to figure out ways of coping with it. Although the focus of this book is family communication and interaction, it's important to realize that outside stress factors – such as work and school pressures – all have a way of creeping into the house and affecting family relationships.

As I've read and listened to various experts speak, one thing that always strikes me is how people always seem to address stress like it's a modern phenomena. They're always talking about the overwhelming stresses on the "modern" family. Like it wasn't stressful for ancient men to worry everyday that their hunt would come up empty, or that one of their children would be carried off by some large snaggle-toothed, shaggy-haired predator? Or it wasn't stressful for families who never knew when the Vikings would show up and loot their villages? Or in the not-so-distant past, when parents were afraid they would be hauled off to debtor's prison if the crops failed? My point is that stress is just a natural part of the human condition – there has always been stress on families, and we need to learn how to deal with it in a natural, everyday manner.

I think one the most important things to remember as we discuss stress is that we will always have a certain amount of stress. We have to accept that fact and then move on to the next thing, which is how we will deal with that stress within our own families, and not let it get so overwhelming that it affects our ability to function as healthy families.

When our kids were little, our families' biggest stress came with either lack of time and having no or little help. I'll never forget the day when Caitlin, then 5 years old, her three younger siblings, and I were getting everyone in the car – late again for something I am sure. As I was strapping the younger ones in, I overheard Caitlin say to herself, "Caitlin do this, Caitlin do that…" My goodness, I thought, I was stressing her out! So, I ended up giving her a "Queen for a Day" once a month where I waited on her for the day as a thank you for all of her big sister help.

My biggest stress when the kids were little was getting to places on time! It seems I was always yelling for them to hurry up or I was frantic getting them ready so we could get out of the house! I finally came up with the best stress cure! *Backwards day!* It was easy to execute, and has high-perceived fun value. I would tell the kids about it the night before to get them all excited. The idea was that for backwards day you had to come to breakfast with your clothes already on, walk to the kitchen backwards, say good night as you came in the kitchen and I would put their cereal in their juice cups and their juice in their cereal bowls! It was easy and fun and it never failed – the kids and I were walking backwards out of the house ahead of schedule!

# Financial Stress

> "Coping with the stress and hardships of a reduced income is not easy. Easy answers and quick cures are not available. If you remember that you are the same person as before, regrouping and adapting will be easier. Maintain control of your situation by reducing and prioritizing spending, making decisions, carrying out your plan, and minimizing anxiety. These steps will help you cope with today as well as strengthen and prepare you and your family for the future."
>
> Wilma Schuh, Joyce E. Jones, and
> Doris "Katey" Walker, Cooperative Extension
> Service, Kansas State University,
> *Making Ends Meet Part 2: Coping With Stress*

**QUOTES**

Unexpected and rapid changes like losing a job, experiencing a bad year on the farm or family business operation, an injury that keeps you unable to work for a while, or even overwhelming debt can result in tremendous stress, and can also result in feelings of reduced self-worth.

Our family made a life choice to give up the corporate income we were used to in order to pursue our dream of helping to strengthen families. We sold our home, lived off of our savings and gave up paychecks for two years! We learned first hand how these pressures can affect a family - from short fuses and tempers rising to family members not communicating and just feeling the overall pressures that our life was not in sync. We never talked about money issues with the kids, but it is amazing how your attitude can spread stress throughout the house. We had to be very conscious of it and keep the lines of communication open first and foremost between Neal and myself and then with the kids. Luckily, we think we caught ourselves early on, but it is something we are continuously monitoring.

When you find yourself in the middle of a financial crisis, maintaining control is important. Concentrate your efforts on keeping your attitude, your family, and your body as strong as possible. If you're dealing with a sudden reduction in income, you must cope with this major worry as well as with the daily reminders of unpaid bills and needs for clothing, medical treatment, or school supplies. You need to try to recognize and control the minor situations that increase your stress level. For example, postponing minor stresses over which you have control may free up the energy you need for responding to the huge stress of your financial difficulties.

Here are some quick tips on how to deal with minor financial stress:

**IDEA**

✔ **Don't panic!**
    You can still control your financial situation, if you plan carefully.

✔ **Communicate.**
    You need to sit down and analyze your financial priorities and talk with your family about what you will do. Don't bottle this stress up and keep it a secret, the family needs to know when money is tight!

✔ **Don't default on payments.**
    Explain the situation to your creditors and work out adjustments. As long as you're making even the smallest of payments to your creditors on a regular basis, it will keep your accounts out of the hands of the collection agencies.

✔ **Make some sacrifices**

You'll need to change your style of living at least temporarily, so that you will still be able to provide the essentials like food, shelter and health care.

# Get Help With Your Finances

"For starters, make a list of your basic monthly expenses, including food, utilities, house payments, insurance, car expenses, clothing, taxes, debt payment and entertainment. Balance this against your income. Now you have some hard figures about the gap between what you have and what you need. Sometimes money problems can be averted just by setting a realistic budget and sticking to it. You'll certainly be in more control of your finances than someone who knows only that more money goes out than comes in."

Mary J. Stephenson, Associate Professor and Family Resource Management Specialist, Cooperative Extension Service, University of Maryland System.

**QUOTES**

After you analyze your situation and if your expenses are just hopelessly out of balance with your income, get outside help. Try Consumer Credit Counseling Services, a national nonprofit organization that provides free or low-cost advice to people who need to improve their financial situation. They're in your phone book. You can also see if your bank, credit union or your company provides financial counseling.

There are also community service organizations such as family service agencies and religious service agencies, and they're also in your phone book.

Just taking some sort of action toward controlling your finances can provide enormous stress relief all by itself. It's very hard to feel in control of your life when you have big money worries – and loss of control will lead to increased stress for every member of your family. Just remember that the key to decreasing financial stress is to take some steps – any steps – to getting the situation under control.

When the financial situation is dire, and you're down to your last few bucks, one slightly comforting factor to remember that it's almost impossible to starve to death in America; no matter how bad things get, there are always government agencies and charities that will see to it that your family gets – at the very least – the things they need to stay alive, like food, shelter, clothing and medical attention. It may hurt your pride to accept charity, but just remember that you're lucky enough to live in a country that will provide at least the basics if you find yourself completely down and out.

# We're Both Working and Completely Stressed Out

**QUOTES**

"Work stress was suggested… to be more important in determining the self-esteem of mothers than fathers, while family stress appeared to be more important in determining depression for fathers than mothers. Overall, the family stressors resulting in depression were different for mothers and fathers; dual-earner fathers reported depression due to lack of spousal support or family role insignificance, whereas dual-earner mothers were sensitive to a lack of task sharing."

Neala S. Schwartzberg, Ph.D., North Shore Child and Family Guidance Center, in
*Dual-Earner Families: The Importance of Work Stress and Family Stress for Psychological Well-Being*

My scenario is that I stopped working when Caitlin was born and then went back to work after our second child, Maggie, was born. I worked for one year, essentially because we were living above our means. We found out fast that that was not for us! We preferred to live exactly within our means so I could stay at home. So, we spent a year going through the stresses and guilt-factors that many dual-earner families go through!

I found out a few things in that year in the world of dual income families. First off, there are the basic things like divvying up the housework in a fair manner when you're both working. You and your spouse will have to work out a reasonable division of labor, or you're just begging for added stress when one partner feels resentment at shouldering more than their fair share of work.

Unless you have a trusted family friend or relative that will be watching your child, you also need to figure out what to do about daycare for younger kids. Finding the appropriate daycare can also take a lot of the stress out of the situation – if you feel comfortable with where your wee ones are, at least you won't be stressing on this 24/7. Choosing the right daycare is not really an easy thing to do. While there are many facilities that look nice on the outside, it's much more important to look at the quality of what's on the inside. Neal and I spent many days and evenings visiting and reading up on local day care centers.

Here are several tips that can help you decide which daycare is best for your child:

**EXAMPLE**

✔ **Count heads**
Know the ratio of workers to children. There should be enough staff on hand throughout the day to ensure that the children have personal attention and care.

✔ **Find out How They Handle Things**
It is essential that your child gets the appropriate discipline when he does something wrong. If there is not enough supervision, he may grow used to doing whatever he wants and try the same tactics at home. Talk to the staff to see how they handle tough situations. You will feel better knowing that someone who truly cares is looking after your child's well-being.

✔ **Child proof**
Keeping track of a multitude of children is not easy. Find out what steps the center takes to minimize the risk of accidents. It is important that there is staff with the children at all times. Although not all accidents are due to negligence, accidents on the playground or in the classroom are less likely to happen if there is close supervision.

✔ **Gourmet or M&Ms**
Some day cares require that you bring in your child's food

everyday, but for those that don't, checking into the food served is crucial. Ask if the meals are nutritional and varied. Also, you should know how often meals or snacks are offered to the kids. If you visit around a meal time, you may even be able to see the food for yourself. You can feel assured that your child's nutritional needs are being met.

✔ **Dollars and Sense**

Choose a quality daycare that is within your budget. It will add to your stress if you send your child to a facility you can't afford. Also, just because a daycare is expensive doesn't necessarily mean it is a great place for your child. Some of the best centers are very reasonably priced.

✔ **Almost home**

Getting your kid to the daycare will be much less stressful if it is nearby. You will find the familiarity and convenience to be comforting to you and your child.

✔ **Romper room**

Ask about what kind of activities the children are involved in. Find out how often the children are allowed to go outside and what kind of playground is available. Playtime is very positive in the health growth of a child. You can feel confident that your child is in a healthy and beneficial atmosphere.

✔ **Sticky fingers**

While touring the center look to see how sanitary the place is. Are the bathrooms kept clean and is the kitchen scrubbed? Also, ask if the staff has been trained in CPR, first aid, preventing communicable diseases, and other health concerns. If your state has a certification program, look for this when choosing the daycare. This helps to immediately eliminate centers that are not on top of things.

✔ **Peer pals**

Find out the ages of most of the other children at the daycare. If your child is seven, you don't want to place her in a center that has mostly toddlers. Make sure she has peers close to her own age. Her playmates will make her experience much more enjoyable.

✔ **Staff rapport**

Watch the staff at the daycare center while they are relating to the kids. You can see what type of rapport they will have with your child. It is important that the teachers show interest in the children and that the kids show respect for the staff. With the right supervision, the interactions your child has at daycare can be a valuable influence on her development.

✔ **Talk to other parents**

We would try to be at daycares at drop off and pick up to both watch and talk to the parents. I still think word of mouth is the best advertising. Get names of families no longer using the facility and call them and talk about the day care.

Adapted from The University of Michigan,
Faculty and Staff Assistance Program

By having a list of guidelines to use when finding a daycare, you can eliminate some of the stress you're feeling about both parents working. When you drop off your child at the daycare center, you can feel happy that you made the right decision. Finding a daycare doesn't have to be stressful. You can make a great decision for your child by using the above tips.

I would also add that, although we all like to avoid making major changes, your childcare decision does not have to be permanent. Continually evaluate the extent to which your daycare arrangement best serves your child. All children will require some adjustment to their new setting and schedule, but once your child is settled in make sure that she is reasonably happy, continuing to grow and thrive, and doesn't give you indication that she feels unsafe or harmed while at daycare. Examine her behavior at home for negative influences that you would rather not expose her to (e.g., profane language, hitting, etc.)

You need to have realistic expectations about what daycare can provide, but don't ever settle for an arrangement that just doesn't seem right... no matter how convenient or affordable it is. There are always other options. Some people prefer hiring a nanny to work in the home, some prefer large daycare centers, others choose small groups out of someone's house, and some prefer academically oriented pre-schools for children two and older. It is worth the time to carefully investigate all of your options, ask everyone you know who has children for their recommendations, and then continue to evaluate the choices you make. Always have a back-up plan. Where and with whom you entrust your child is a huge decision with many potential consequences. Take your time!

# Single Parent & Divorce Stress Issues

**QUOTES**

> "Since 1970, the number of children living in a single parent family has doubled. In fact, statistics from 1992 indicate that single parent families represent 30% of U.S. households, while 25% represent two parent households. Based on current trends, there are predictions that upwards of 70% of children born since 1980 will spend some time living in a single parent home before their 18th birthday. *These children are not doomed to failure.*"
>
> Shellee Darnell, family Therapist, in
> *How To be The Best Single Parent You Can*

Raising kids and maintaining a healthy family life can be stressful enough, but when you find yourself handling it all by yourself it can get really, really rough.  And while happily married couples can never understand what you're going through, take heart in the fact that there are lots of single parents out there raising wonderful, loving kids. You're not really alone in this!  If you take steps along the way to manage the unique stress of single parenting, you'll find that you're doing a much better job than you ever thought you could!

While I don't need to tell the single parents who are reading this book anything about the challenges they're facing, here's a few words for those of us who come in contact with the children of single parents everyday. If we all think about this a little bit, maybe we can help as a community to lower the stress of single parents.

Whether or not the single parent family exists as a result of divorce, death or that the parents were never married, it's obvious that the child had nothing at all to do with it. However, it's the kids who often have to pay the price! Just think about how you would feel if it was your kid who sits on the bench because they missed practices while visiting the other parent, or who comes home crying from school, sad when he doesn't know who to make a Father's Day card for because his father died. As teachers, coaches, neighbors, family, and friends we all need to be a bit more sensitive and compassionate and recognize that single parents are working just as hard (if not harder) as we are to raise good kids too!

Here are some tips to help relieve stress for single parents: (Some of these should be recommended for *all* parents)

**IDEA**

✔ **Organize A Co-Op of Single Parents**

Although this is a lot of work at the beginning, it will help immensely when trying to iron out the scheduling conflicts between work and your child's activities. Co-ops can help with car-pooling, baby sitting, play groups, buying food in bulk and just offering you the support of others in your situation. Good places to begin your search for interested single parents are your child's school, daycare, sports teams or a local chapter of Parents Without Partners.

✔ **Plan ahead for sick days**

A virus or extended illness for the single parent who has a pre-schooler can be disastrous. Try to plan ahead for these times, and have several sitters lined for emergencies.

✔ **Share Household Chores**

You can't do it all yourself, and your kids need to build a sense of responsibility anyway. Be sure to give children housework chores based on their developmental stages and capabilities – children learn the valuable lesson of self-dependence when they are given chores within their abilities. Teach your children now so they can survive when out on their own: both our boys and girls share laundry, dishes, garbage, cleaning and sewing duties in our home. Watch out though: avoid the temptation to put too much responsibility on the kids. (Remember poor Caitlin!) Most libraries carry current parenting books and magazines that offer sound advice on age appropriate chores; check one out and read up on this.

✔ **Remember your extended family**
Family members can be a godsend for the single parent, but some single parents view seeking support as a sign of weakness or inadequacy. Don't be silly! If family members want to be a positive part of your new family unit, they may offer help with childcare, food preparation, and grant moral support.

✔ **Don't forget to rest**
You need to have time for yourself to refresh, energize yourself or rest. Finding time for yourself can be time alone to listen to music, read a book, visit with friends, attend a support group or indulge in any other activities you enjoy. You need contact with people your own age! Physical, mental, and emotional exhaustion is a part of any parenting situation, and yet it's twice as bad for the single parent. Try to set aside a few minutes of quiet time during your day. It can be just for 15 minutes before the kids get up or 15 minutes after they go to bed. (This is important for all of us to do!)

✔ **Don't take lashing out personally**
Your kids are stressed about this whole situation too. It's normal for a child to have deep feelings, or even a fantasy relationship, regarding a parent who is rarely around (or entirely absent). Remember that kids are prone to lash out at those they feel safest with. Just ride it out, and then spend a little time telling your kids how much you love them and that you're grateful to have them as your children.

✔ **If you decide to date, keep it private for a while**

It's not necessary, or even healthy, to introduce each person you date to your children. Some dates are just dates, some are the beginning of a relationship, but if you parade everyone you date in front of the kids you're just bound to cause confusion. Wait until the relationship becomes somewhat serious before introductions are made. Never forget that most kids are always hoping that you'll somehow, someday be reunited with the missing parent anyway. Being sensitive to their feelings can save you a lot of stress in the long run.

For the single parent, the idea of family meals and meetings are even more important. With all of the responsibilities you're shouldering, it can be hard to find the time to really connect. But you need to make the extra effort to schedule at least one family meal and meeting a week. If you do that, and try some of the *Family Table Time* Exercises I've been suggesting at the end of the preceding chapters, you'll be able to see problems looming ahead and keep the lines of communication open between you and your kids.

# Parents Caring for Parents: the Sandwich Generation

More and more parents are finding out that they will soon need to begin caring for their own parents as well. Today, statistics say we will spend more time taking care of our parents than we did taking care of our children. In addition to the complexities of normal family life, they realize that the parents who had always taken care of them may now need a little help of their own. So now, instead of being the older generation in a house, parents find themselves in the curious position of being the middle generation. Our parents are not living with us but we know the importance of being there for them as they age. Our stress comes from not being in the same town, and the guilt on that alone can be stressful. Many people have a little bit of a problem when they're put into the uncomfortable position of having to make the rules that their own parents must follow, but this is essential. Parents must run their own households!

While a multi-generational experience can be wonderful for your kids, there are also whole new sets of stresses and demands put on a family when "new" adults become part of the immediate family structure.

Here are some guidelines to avoid sources of stress when setting up a multi-generational household:

**IDEA**

✔ **Make sure everyone knows all the rules.**
Include everything – eating schedules, cleanup responsibilities, space arrangements, laundry duties, transportation, and when the house is to be quiet in the evening. Review the rules from time to time at your family meals and meetings to accommodate changing circumstances and to keep the lines of communication open. Expect all to abide by the middle-generation's values while they are under that roof.

✔ **Prepare a long-range financial plan.**
If you have college students, or adults returning home, or a frail parent, you will need to work out a detailed plan about who is financially responsible for what. Keep detailed records and have a very specific budget. This is important in allocating resources as well as in preparing taxes.

✔ **Use available community programs and services.**
Contact your local or state agency on aging to find out about available programs. Use elder day care if possible. Often a special bus will pick up an older adult and drop them off later. Get your parent involved in a local senior center. One of the most important measures of health in an elderly individual is the number of social

contacts that a person has. This kind of contact is especially important for a widowed parent who is feeling isolated.

✔ **Respect one another's privacy.**
All generations should have their own lives, independent of each other. It is important to define personal boundaries and personal space. All family members need to work on this. This approach requires constant monitoring of events and family members' behaviors and feelings.

✔ **Remember That You're The Boss, as Well as The Mediator**
For example, Grandma may have to be pacified in regard to her concerns about the children's dress or their unwillingness to attend church on Sunday mornings. On the other hand, Grandma's inflexibilities and seemingly outdated values may need to be interpreted at critical moments to the younger generation.

✔ **Don't neglect your own family to take care of your parent.**
Don't ignore whatever seems to be functioning to "oil the squeaky wheel." Sometimes family members who seem to be doing fine really are not. Your family meals and meetings will help you keep a handle on this.

✔ **Make caring for your parent a responsibility for the whole family.**
This is not just your job. Your siblings, as well as their children, should be made to understand that they need to help out emotionally, physically and financially.

✔ **Make everyone in the family aware of any problems.**
Full explanations are important. If an adult has Alzheimer's, for instance, it can be very frightening and very challenging.

✔ **If a parent moves into your home, that person should have their own room and phone.**

Always discuss expectations in advance. Are you going to have to take time off work to care for the parent? What are other family members' responsibilities? The family should continue regular activities as much as possible.

✔ **Take the time for self-renewal.**

You must continue with your life, with your job. You are not good to anyone if you are overburdened with guilt about not doing enough. Highly stressed individuals are less effective and less efficient. You cannot totally put your life on hold.

✔ **Take time for your marriage.**

Neal and I think this is very important for all couples, even if grandparents are not in the home. Not only is it great for our relationship but we love it when our kids see us still have a life together and hear them joke about our date nights! Go out once a week with your spouse, doing something you both enjoy. Make a special effort to increase the amount of intimate time together. Don't let your marriage become a victim of the emotional fallout from the pressures of a multi-generational household.

Adapted From Herbert G. Lingren,
Extension Family Life Specialist,
University of Nebraska, in
*The Sandwich Generation: A Cluttered Nest*

# You Need to Know When the Stress is Too Much for You to Handle

> "Families are often the source of their own healing. Sometimes, all that is needed is to gather and talk as a total unit about the stress, to talk and listen and struggle with the problem. If this is not sufficient, you may need to seek help from a church, mental health center, or other counseling agency."
>
> **Pauline Boss**, Family Social Science,
> College of Human Ecology,
> University of Minnesota

**QUOTES**

Sometimes, despite all the steps you have taken to reduce, manage, or control stress professional assistance may be needed to help you find ways to cope and find new solutions. It's important to know when and where to seek help. Professional help may come from mental health agencies, lay groups, community agencies, family physicians and religious advisors. All of these people can help you deal with extreme stress.

Here are some tips that your stress is getting out of control and you need to seek help:

✔ You're depressed most of the time. (Signs of depression are difficulty sleeping, or sleeping constantly; crying often; feeling that you don't want to do anything; constant fatigue; unreasonable fears; inability to concentrate; and change in appetite.)

✔ You start to show violence toward your family. .

✔ You have thoughts of suicide.

**WARNING**

✔ You start thinking that a divorce would solve your problems.

✔ You begin to discipline your children too harshly.

✔ You're constantly negative about yourself or family members.

✔ You hear voices or see things.

✔ You start to drink more alcohol, especially drinking in the morning. Other danger signs are hiding your drinking, or you become mean while drinking.

✔ You aren't comfortable talking to anyone. You isolate yourself socially.

✔ You find yourself lying to people constantly.

✔ You start lying to yourself.

✔ You have panic attacks, accompanied by a fast pulse and difficulty breathing.

✔ You notice your children are starting to have disciplinary and behavioral problems, getting into trouble with the law, or are acting strangely.

If you see some of these symptoms in yourself or your family, it's probably time to find a trained, skilled professional to help you and your family. A family counselor can help you handle your fears and adjust to your present situation. Don't be worried that you won't be able to afford their services; most cities or counties make these services available at low cost or no charge if you are unable to pay.

# Relieving Stress Exercises

Here are some quick tips for relieving stress:

✔ Get physical! Increase your exercise in any way that appeals to you.

✔ Limit your caffeine intake

✔ Get plenty of rest

✔ Listen to relaxing music and stress reduction tapes alone or as a family

✔ Schedule time off from your worries – plan activity times when worry is off limits.  Then plan brief periods of time when you will actively think about what is stressing you so that you can brainstorm solutions and decide what you will do to change the stressor, change the way you think about the stressor, or change the way you are coping with stress.  Do not allow yourself to sit and worry endlessly without a problem-solving focus.

**IDEA**

# What Have We Learned?

After reading this chapter, you should better understand some of the ways that you can reduce stress or avoid introducing new stress into your family's life. You've got some tips and tools to help guide your family away from harmful stress and some strategies to help you when you find yourself faced with unavoidable stressful situations.

Chapter Fourteen

# Chapter Fifteen
## Group Effort

## With a Little Help From Our Family and Friends

I can't believe that it's been four years since Neal and I and the kids came up with the idea that eventually became *Family Table Time*. It's been a group effort all the way, from our initial family discussions on that fateful car trip to Chicago, to the nineteen families that helped us test our original concept out, and to all the help and encouragement we've received from the Bush family – most notably Governor Jeb Bush of Florida and former First Lady, Barbara Bush.

We've seen how important meals with the family can be. When the demands of "corporate life" caused us to question what was really important, we resolved to take our family back – and we decided that dinnertime was going to be the place. To make the time together more meaningful and fun, we eventually developed *Family Table Time* – a weekly family meeting kit that's simple, practical and fun. One of my favorite features is a keepsake tablecloth that all family members can write and draw their family memories down on. What began as an idea to help our family re-knit has become a way for all families to plan activities, build values and strengthen family unity.

In this chapter, we'd like to share with you what people have said about their experiences, some of what it has meant to us, and our vision for what this can mean for families all over the world.

I'd like to start with some comments from the people who mean the most to me, my own family.

> "We started when I was in 4th grade so I probably remember the most, what things use to be like. But it was hard to start and hard to have conversations, I'd give just quick one word answers to my parents questions like, 'How was your day?' and I'd just say, 'Good.' So, I guess the biggest thing is just being able to communicate and talk easily. The mission statement is very powerful for me. We wrote one in the beginning and we have expanded it – we heard this song about Jesus telling you thank you when you get to heaven so we added that to our mission statement because we liked that thought a lot. It just helps me when I am faced with choices, to go back to the mission statement and think about what I really want to do with my life, and so it gives me direction."
>
> Caitlin Kimball

> "I love looking back at the past years' tablecloths and laughing about stuff we wrote and spelled wrong. It's fun to see what was important to us before... It's fun – we really treat each other differently now – just take it one meal at a time. The best is getting time to say what you are thinking and finding out what's going on with everyone else."
>
> Maggie Kimball

"I like the leader part, especially being the leader when I get to choose the meal and topic and game. The compliments, these have improved, in the beginning it would be like well, I guess you didn't hit me that hard today – and now we really mean it! So, for example this week I told Jimmy that I noticed that he included me when his friend came over to play and that made me feel good."

Kyle Kimball

"I like eating together and making the meal. I think that when we work on a value each week it helps make our family closer – like "You First," letting other's go first, like when we get on the bus in the morning."

Jimmy Kimball

# What Other Families Are Saying

**EXAMPLE**

"It is amazing, it is the only night during the week, where our son, who is autistic, *comes* to the table and actually enjoys and takes part in our family meal and meeting!"
Bill and Patti Calderara, Parents
Connecticut

"This has been a blessing for our family by providing a fun activity that brings all of the family members together to eat, pray, listen, talk, and build a family values foundation for our home."
Ross Hawkins, Parent
Oregon

"This is a great tool for families to help them communicate and focus on the important stuff, 'each other'."
Mike and Kate Flores, Parents
Pennsylvania

"We have more fun at dinner time now that we have made it a priority! Lots of conversation and values shared, we love it!"
Mike and Elaine Bagley, Parents
North Carolina

"After years of sitting around the table and struggling with one word answers from our kids, now we have the lively art of conversation. We're finally talking as a family!"
Peter and Donna Urbain, Parents
Illinois

We've been having one meal a week with our family meeting for years now. But one of our test families in Chicago had always been intimidated by having family meetings. They said they read how important they are, but never really knew how to go about having one.

The information we provide talked them through it and now they take part in them on regular basis. This family of six, with a 13 year-old boy, 10 year-old boy, 7 year-old girl and 3 year-old girl, has improved their communication greatly. The father says he now makes it a point to be home for all the dinners because of the great dynamic they have at dinner and that it carries over into their lives.

We watched one of their meetings and we were blown away with the connectedness of the family. One part of the meeting is about complimenting each other. The three year old, as well as the other kids, really got into this. She gave compliments and if she didn't receive one from each family member she requested it!

When our family started this process of complimenting it was a disaster. Our kids didn't understand how to give compliments. But after a couple of weeks of coaching and leading by example, it has become our family's favorite part (outside of the dessert). Our 7-year old son stated that when we come to this part of the meeting it is like "flowers coming off of our tongues!"

One of our moms mentioned that having an agenda sheet on the refrigerator has been so helpful. In the past, when the kids came home from school they were able to tell her their news right away. Now after they tell her, she reminds them to write it on the agenda sheet so they can be sure to share it with the family at the dinner table.

Another family of five, with a 14 year-old boy, 10-year old girl and 5 year-old girl has enjoyed the process as well. The father and son's communication has also improved greatly. At first the son thought this was a "geeky" idea but now he loves it the most. His reasoning, "I am busy about six nights a week and I know at least one night each week I can sit down and find out what everybody else is doing." His dad says he has become a better listener. Before, the family had run with "what father says goes... no discussion." Now, he still feels the parents have the final say but now he can hear where his kids are coming from.

The tablecloths of each of the families are beautiful! They all have their own personalities and expressions, memories via words and drawings... mission statements that clearly express who and what their family stands for – all in bright colors that will stand the test of time. What a wonderful memory the families will have to look back on! Imagine bringing the family tablecloths out to show their children and grandchildren at a far off reunion!

Another family of five, with a 6 year-old girl, a 5 year-old girl and a 4 year-old boy, said they would try the process for our sake, thinking that they didn't need it yet. They were surprised with how much they got out of it. Their tablecloth and meetings have a different dynamic, but the time together is powerful. They're setting a precedent and the communication lines are open.

The mother told me, "My kids love talking about themselves, at this age they love to tell the tiniest details of their lives and for them to have a place where they know they will be heard will only benefit them in there older years. Keep them talking and keep listening and my family will stay strong. We have wonderful meetings, and our tablecloth is filled with drawings of things that are important to my children... we will treasure this forever and look forward to seeing how the dynamics of our tablecloths and meetings change over the years."

# What the Experts Are Saying

"There is solid research that shows that not sharing family meals can have a significant impact on kids. There are numerous studies and surveys that all point in the same direction. When families don't get together regularly over the dinner table the kids are more prone to depression and drug use, don't eat as well and don't do as well in school. A 1994 survey of 2000 high school seniors by Lou Harris and Associates, for example, found that students who regularly ate dinner with their families four or more times a week scored better in a battery of academic tests than those who ate family dinners three or fewer times a week."

Cindy Reishus, chair of the
Nutrition Education Network

**QUOTES**

Over the past few years, we have shared *Family Table Time* via conventions (East Coast Family Conference, United Nations/Preventing Violence and Promoting a Culture of Caring and Peace in our Schools) and workshops (local churches and family- based organizations) across the Eastern seaboard of the United States. So it's very gratifying to hear experts in the field endorsing our ideas, and telling us that we're doing something good for families in general. It's our dream, as a family, to share the importance of families eating meals together.

# Making it a Group Effort

Our goal is definitely achievable, and simple. We'd like to encourage parents and families to start local support groups based around the people you know in your neighborhoods, schools, churches, sports teams, book clubs, etc. This will help you help each other share best

**TOGETHER**

practices for parenting, become connected to new families, and understand the personality and moral fabric of the parents/families that your children engage with on a regular basis.

There are already quite a few kinds of parent action groups, usually organized by parents for parents, which meet and discuss issues, help each other with tips, and work together to effect change not only in their own families but in the community. We'd like to see people talking about the importance of family meals and meetings in settings like parent action groups. My list of groups is adapted from some research by the U.S. Department of Health and Human Services. You might already be involved in groups like these, as they tend to fit into one of the following models:

## Parent Peer Groups:

These are centered on the friendship circle of a group of young people. Remember how we had advised you to get to know your kid's friends parents? These are very informal groups of two or three parents which meet periodically at a member's house to discuss parenting issues, or larger groups which meet to share concerns and discuss solutions. These groups of parents usually agree among themselves on curfews, party rules and behavior expectations for their young people.

## Parent Classroom/School Groups

These are made up of parents of young people who attend the same school or are in the same classroom at school. This type of group focuses on the education of parents and kids that attend a particular school and typically meets at the school in the evenings. This type of group can be particularly effective in agreeing on curfews, acceptable party behavior and supervision and chaperoning strategies. Many parent classroom groups work for change in school and school district policies regarding extra-curricular activities and may even agree on the style of clothing to be worn to school by their young people. Some very structured groups have organized the schools through home rooms so that every parent is reached with information. Others have become involved in working directly with the schools on codes, guidelines and policies. PTA's are examples of this type of group and they may be reached for assistance in organizing this type of parent group.

**National Congress of Parents and Teachers (PTA)**
330 North Wabash Avenue, Ste. 2100
Chicago, IL 60611-3690
800-307-4782
(312) 670-6782
(312) 670-6783 (fax)
Email: info@pta.org
Web site: www.pta.org

## Parent Neighborhood Groups:

These groups may meet in homes, schools, churches or other neighborhood facilities and are usually started by parents wanting to make changes in the neighborhood in which they live. They may deal with issues such as identifying safe houses for children who need somewhere to go in an emergency, or agreeing to generally "watch out" for neighborhood children. Many parent neighborhood groups work with their local police departments, setting up neighborhood watch groups to increase security. Families have been reached through informal coffee meetings or door-to-door solicitation as well as neighborhood get-togethers such as ball games, cook-outs, etc. These groups also have the advantage of involving senior citizens living in the area.

## Parent Support Groups:

These are made up of parents who are having difficulty with their kids. Many parents can find help and support in meeting and working with other parents who are experiencing the same problems. Such groups may be informally structured or may be organized through local mental health or hospital programs. These groups tend top deal with specific issues like children with illnesses, or substance abuse problems. There are several national support groups which began as local groups, and expanded as more and more people benefited from involvement with them.

## Community-Wide Parent Action Groups

These are organizations addressing several different community areas such as parent and school education, legislation, drug paraphernalia availability and court watching. In some areas, several established community parent groups have joined together to form a Community Parent Coalition. See if there is in one of these in you community. Entire community involvement can be a very powerful way to change the environment in which young people mature.

## Grandparent Groups

These are rapidly growing in number as grandparents are taking a more active role in raising their grandchildren. It is estimated that nearly 4 million children live in a household headed by a grandparent and for over 1.5 million of these children no parent is present, so the grandparent assumes the role of parent. Census Bureau information shows that grandparent-headed families cross all socioeconomic and ethnic groups. Here are some places you might want to call for a little guidance if you're thinking about starting a grandparents group.

**American Association of Retired Persons (AARP)**
AARP Grandparent Information Center
601 E Street, NW
Washington, DC 20049
Phone: (202) 434-2296
Fax: (202) 434-6466

**Grandparents Reaching Out (GRO)**
141 Glen Summer Road
Holbrook, NY 11741
Phone: (516) 447-0062
Fax: (516) 472-4450

**Informed Families Education Center**
2490 Coral
Miami, FL 33145
Phone: (305) 856- 4886
Fax: (305) 856-4815
info@informedfamilies.org

## Fatherhood Groups:

These groups are also growing in number, with over 2,000 grassroots groups alone. These groups have organized in response to the growing numbers of fathers wanting to be more effective in helping raise their children. Here are some places you might want to call for a little guidance if you're thinking about starting a fatherhood group:

**The National Center for Fathering**
10200 W. 75th Street
Shawnee Mission, KS 66204
Phone: (800) 593-3237

**The Fatherhood Project**
The Families and Work Institute
330 Seventh Avenue, 14th Floor
New York, NY 10001
Fax: (212) 465-8637

**The National Fatherhood Initiative**
One Bank Street, Suite 160
Gaithersburg, MD 20878
Phone: (301) 948-0599 or
(800) 790-DADS
Fax: (301) 948-4325
Email: NF11995@aol.com

**Family First**
PO Box 2882
Tampa, FL 33601
Phone:  (813) 222-8300
www.familyfirst.net

## Single-Parent Groups:

These are organizations which deal with issues specific to single parent families, such as legal, social and spiritual concerns and the problems associated with being divorced, never-married, or separated parents. These groups also have a national organization that can get you started forming groups on a local basis.

**Parents Without Partners International, Inc. (PWP)**
401 North Michigan Avenue
Chicago, IL 60611-4267
Phone: (312) 644-6610
Fax: (312) 321-5194
Web site: www.parentswithoutpartners.org

If you are already involved with a group like I've listed above, you may want to start discussing family meals and meeting with them. Or, you may wish to join a group like one of those above and begin to have discussions with them. Other parents who are in the same situation as you often have very helpful hints.

# Family Meals Are Validated by Bush Family

The Bush Family is one "group" that has been very helpful in getting the word out about family meals and meetings.

When President Bush was in Orlando in 2001, the infamous encounter happened when Neal, Caitlin, Maggie and I went to see him. The girls wrote out a question in hopes that they would be able to ask it of the President. (We had heard that he was going to be taking questions.) We were seated way in the back and found out that only people in the front section were to be involved in the question asking part. We went up to the gate and mentioned that we had a question and how could we get it asked. I guess they felt for the girls because they called over a White House Staffer, and he said he would see what he could do. He found four empty seats, the next thing we knew we were inside, about 40 feet from the President's podium!

Of course, President Bush was great but what was even better was that he picked on the girls when they raised their hand! Both girls stood up and Caitlin sounded a little nervous when she said hello. The whole transcript of this give and take between the President and our girls is included in the first chapter of our book.

After the meeting ended, our family was able to shake the President's hand, which was quite a thrill. I told him this was my family and he gave me a wonderful look and head nod as if to say, "You should be very proud!" After he walked by, his brother, our Governor, Jeb Bush came by and shook our hands. He stopped to talk with us, mentioning the organization CASA, Center on Addiction and Substance Abuse, which also promotes family dinners and how one of the biggest deterrence for drug use is families eating meals together! We told him we were familiar with CASA, and knew his wife, Columba, was on the board and that we were in touch with them regarding our project,

*Family Table Time*. He high-fived Neal!  At that point we told Gov. Bush more about *Family Table Time*, and gave him some information that we also mailed to the White House some days previously – he promised he would read it!

Wow! The girls got whisked away to be interviewed by the local press regarding their experience. We couldn't believe our day. We went home in awe! Picked up the boys (who didn't believe us at first), and sat down to a late family meal.  The phone rang and Caitlin picked it up. (Of course we had just finished, we don't answer the phone during dinner!)We heard her say thank you and then a look of shock on her face as she mouthed to us "It's the governor!" She asked if she could put him on speaker and we all talked to him!

Governor Bush had called to commend the girls on their courage and their great question. He also wanted to talk more about *Family Table Time*. He loved it! We spent about 20 minutes on the phone with him, and he is really a wonderful, down-to-earth guy who wants to make a difference.  He invited us up to Tallahassee to talk more about how we can use *Family Table Time* to help families.  We ended the phone conversation knowing that we were going to meet with him to talk more about helping families and that he saw a great need for the *Family Table Time* tool and wanted to get it out on family's tables.

After that call, we were invited up to the Governors office and explained the entire process. Our relationship with the Governor began. Subsequently, Neal was appointed to The Governor's Transition Task Force to discuss ideas to help make Florida the best place in the world to live and raise a family. Neal was able to share his insights and the principles behind *Family Table Time* with state policy makers at the highest level.  Our ideals fit in perfectly with what the Governor is trying to accomplish:

✔ The Family plan must be well thought out, specific to the situation, realistic, proactive and doable. Focused planning gives the state the potential to achieve long-term prioritized goals while surviving unexpected crises and volatile periods.

✔ To be successful, strategic planning must be an on-going process that determines how the actions of the State of Florida will be focused on accomplishing the long-term goals or vision of the communities.

✔ This "vision" will pull the state forward toward the future and provides the motivation for meeting and overcoming the many challenges facing any family. A vision statement should encompass the state's four-year expectations for primary services, distinctive competencies and features, geographic coverage.

Excerpted from Florida Strategic Plan

All of this positive attention from families in positions of authority has just strengthened our belief that our whole plan of family meals and meetings is something that we need to keep talking about, and to keep exposing to more and more families.

# Chapter Fifteen

# Chapter Sixteen
## Remember Why You Are Doing This

### Achieving Your Goals

"It's important that you allow both yourself and your child to make mistakes. Be consistent. Ask for help when you need it. And reward yourself and your children when you succeed. Parenting can be a magnificent endeavor when you plan to make the most of it."

A. Renee Staton, PhD, LPC, NCC,

in Setting Goals for More Effective Parenting

**QUOTES**

When I look back at all the topics we discussed in the book, and all of the things that I stressed were important, it's easy to see how somebody could get overwhelmed when faced with all of the things they need to think about as a parent. Well, you shouldn't feel like that. You're obviously trying to do the right things for your kids, or you wouldn't still be here with me in Chapter 16!

So, you need to relax a little bit, because you're doing great! Once you're ready to begin opening the door to more open lines of communication with your family, you'll have all the benefits of the tips and guidelines that you read about in this book.

Please just remember that all of this takes time. Your kids aren't going to just open up and start gushing with lovely and insightful conversation the first time you sit down to a family meeting. In fact, it may take quite a few family meetings before you feel like you're getting anywhere at all with it.

Again, relax, you're doing great. The whole idea of family meals and meetings will just take a little time to get accustomed to.

Remember one thing though: this is not a quick fix, and not something you can do whenever it's convenient. You need to commit to having regular meals, and stick to the schedule no matter what! One of the main tenets of this whole deal is constant reinforcement – the more meals and meeting you have, the deeper your messages will sink into your kids' heads!

Don't give up too easily; this will eventually work. And to make it easier for you to actually plan and run family meals and meetings, Neal and I have put together a kit that will get you off and running. The *Family Table Time* Kit is a self-contained kit that has everything in it that you need to begin having family meals and meetings (except the food!) And I promise you that after using this kit for a few weeks, you'll agree with me that it's fun and easy to do.

# Some Tips on How to Make Family Meals Easier

Since the whole point of this one special meal a week thing is to work within your family's busy schedule, you'll need to limit your time in the kitchen as much as possible. So for some of this chapter, we'll focus on how to make quick and nutritional meals.

Here are some simple tips on how to keep good nutritional food on the table while you're getting out of the kitchen as quickly as possible.

**MEAL TIME**

✔ **Combine Cooking and Family Time**
   Spend time with kids at the end of a busy day and get dinner on the table at the same time. It's a great opportunity to catch up with the kids while they learn to be comfortable in the kitchen. Choose tasks that match their ability and that make your job easier such as washing vegetables, wrapping potatoes, getting out ingredients, measuring ingredients, shredding lettuce or setting the table. The added bonus - kids are more likely to eat foods they help prepare.

✔ **Make Chicken Pizza**
   Place boneless, skinless chicken breast in an 8 x 8-inch baking dish. Cover with prepared tomato-basil (or other favorite red sauce). Top with a generous layer of shredded mozzarella cheese. Cover with foil and bake until tender - about 45 minutes at 325 degrees F. Serve with angel hair pasta, salad and whole-grain bread.

✔ **Double Up**
   Make an extra batch when you cook main-dish items such as chili, macaroni and cheese, soups or spaghetti sauce and freeze it. Be sure to date and label each item.

✔ **Serve a Meal in a Potato**
   Baked potatoes are the ultimate convenience food... and they're

nutritious. Bake them in the oven at 375 degrees F for about an hour or in the microwave oven if time is limited. Allow about 7 minutes for a potato. Be sure to pierce them with a fork beforehand. Top them with Italian meat sauce and Parmesan cheese; chili and Cheddar cheese; broccoli, cheese sauce and cooked chicken; or Asian stir-fry vegetables.

✔ **Minimize Cooking time**
Grill, stir-fry or use the microwave as often as possible.

✔ **Think Convenience**
For the goal of good nutrition, the extra cost may be well worth it when it's hot. Shop for pre-cooked items like deli-roasted chicken, or store-prepared casseroles and pastas. Purchase pre-cut and washed vegetables and salads.

✔ **Marinate Meat Before Freezing**
Portion beef, chicken or pork into re-sealable bags. Add your favorite marinade and refrigerate overnight before freezing. Be sure to label and date packages.

✔ **Kid-Pleasing Chicken Tenders**
Coat chicken tenders with barbecue sauce and grill. They're so small they're done in minutes! Serve with potatoes baked on the grill and fresh corn on the cob.

✔ **Keep Milk on the Menu**
Kids need milk 365 days of the year! Serve it with meals and for snacks try flavored milk too. It's as nutritious as white milk.

# Make Grocery Shopping a Family Affair

Shopping may be easier as a solo parental activity, but it can be lots of fun and a great teaching and learning experience for the whole family. You can actually build this time into a supplement to your family meals and meetings. A short while after a meal is the best time to go so that you avoid buying everything off of the shelves when you are hungry and you come back with only what you need.

Spend most of your time in the produce department. Explore the exotic varieties of fruits and veggies and decide as a family which new food you will try this week. When children are included in shopping and they have some say over what to bring home, they are likely to be more interested in the foods you have selected. Who knew that a furry, brown little kiwi could be so much fun?

Here are some quick tips on how to work time spent in the grocery store into part of your whole family meals and meetings experience:

✔ **Enjoy a Rainbow of Colors**
Take advantage of the array of colorful fresh fruits and veggies that are available year round! Look for weekly specials at local farmers' markets or in the produce aisle. Deeply colored fruits and veggies provide essential vitamins, minerals and phytochemicals that promote health and help prevent diseases such as cancer.

✔ **Choose Milk for Calcium**
With so many calcium-fortified juices on the market, it's tempting to substitute them for milk. Calcium-fortified juices and juice drinks don't contain the package of bone-building nutrients provided by milk, including vitamin D and protein.

**FUN FACT**

✔ **Go for the Whole Grains**

Whole grains provide more fiber, vitamins and minerals and other protective substances than their refined cousins. From breads to pastas, the choices are endless. Look for grains such as whole-wheat flour, graham flour, oatmeal, brown rice, whole oats, or barley as the first ingredient on the label.

✔ **Stock Up**

Instead of buying soda, check the dairy case for chocolate and other flavored milks. Kids love these quick, nutritious cold drinks anytime.

✔ **Look for 100%**

When buying juices look for 100 percent on the label. They provide nutrients not found in fruit drinks. Even if it is 100 percent juice, the American Academy of Pediatrics recommends limiting children's juice intake to no more than 4 to 6 ounces for 1 to 6 year-olds and 8 to 12 ounces for 7 to 18 year-olds. Beyond that, give kids great-tasting summer fruits from the produce aisle that provide fiber and other nutrients juices don't.

✔ **Shop for Travel-Friendly Options**

Shop for easy-to-pack, nutritious foods trip when planning trips to the park or for a day trip. Check the dairy case for single-serve yogurt, pudding, string cheese; the produce aisle for "packables" that don't bruise easily and pre- cut veggies; the bakery for bread sticks, bagels, animal crackers, rice cakes and the deli case for protein packed dips such as hummus.

✔ **Make It a Teaching Experience**

Let kids help you make the weekly grocery list, and if they are old enough, organize it by the Food Guide Pyramid. Add some fun to your shopping expedition with games to see who can find foods that fit the right nutritional requirements.

✔ **Let Kids Choose**

An important part of teaching kids to eat nutritious foods is introducing them to new tastes. Let kids choose a new food such as flat bread, a new yogurt flavor, or a new whole-grain cereal to try during the week.

from *Nutrition Exploration:*
*Parents Family Guide To Healthy Eating*

# Universal Tips to Encourage Healthy Eating

Examine the foods in your pantry, fridge, and freezer. What's in your pantry and in your fridge? Whatever we have at home is what we are going to eat. The choices you make during that fateful trip at the grocery store will impact the whole family. If there's a large variety of fresh, delicious fruits and vegetables at home, you'll eat them. If there was a 2-for-1 sale on chips, you'll be eating twice as many chips this week. Look closely at what you are making available for the family.

**MEAL TIME**

If you are preaching that the kids are eating too much junk, ask yourself why there is so much junk food in the house to begin with. Make a variety of nutritious foods available and easy to access at home. Wash and cut up fruits and veggies so they are as easy to grab as a cookie or other convenient snack. Make sure that the healthy selections are visible so that they won't rot in the bottom bin of the fridge because nobody knew they were there.

For the grab and go needs of the family, have boxes of raisins, little bags of baby carrots, nuts, or pretzels available. And don't forget the freezer. Try replacing ice cream with frozen yogurt and sorbets. Frozen entrées are quick and easy, but like fast food they are packed with sodium and sometimes fat that we can all do without. Limit your use as much as possible.

# If You Ban it, They Will Crave it

**WARNING**

Try to avoid making a long list of forbidden foods. There is a research that shows that deprivation can lead to binges. That's why people gorge themselves when they break a diet… for every restriction there is an equal but opposite reaction. Rather than labeling foods as "bad" and never allowing them, aim to teach your children that balance is the key. It is okay to have some special dessert-like treats when you also have eaten some nutritious foods that are good for your body. Everything in moderation and you won't have to worry about your kids sneaking food or lying to you about what they ate at school.

Some of the biggest junk food junkies we know were once kids who were denied any treats. There's a theory called "harm reduction," which is an increasingly popular approach to substance use in adults, and it applies to food as well. The idea is that you know your children are going to occasionally (!) eat non-nutritious foods, so just try to reduce the harm done: limit the amounts and frequency of treats, get them to brush their teeth after sugary snacks, and make sure they stay active to avoid excessive weight gain.

# A Spoon Full of Fun Helps the Fruits and Veggies Go Down

**EXAMPLE**

Lots of children, especially toddlers, respond really well to the added fun of dipping their foods. Make a variety of condiments and dips available and encourage the kids to have fun trying them. Ketchup, honey mustard, duck sauce, ranch dressing, and yogurt are just a few of the things you can experiment with. Try a small muffin pan or ice cube tray as a cute way to offer a large variety. Just like we adults might enjoy a good fondue, children will enjoy the novelty and taste of "dips."

# The One Taste Rule Works

Require that the kids take at least a taste of all of the different foods served. They may be surprised that this week they like the green beans or those nuts and raisins in the salad make it more interesting. Teaching good manners (saying "I don't prefer that" rather than "Gross!") is always a good idea when the taste test goes sour.

**IDEA**

# Get Sneaky

They may dislike carrots but will eat carrot muffins. They may say they detest tomatoes but will eat spaghetti sauce. You can't really taste pureed vegetables that are hidden in a delicious sauce. So, get creative and get a little sneaky!

# You Can't Have Too Many Cooks

Just like the trip to the grocery store, a meal can sometimes be prepared more quickly by a solo adult cook than with junior helpers, but that takes all of the fun out of it. So, on your special family meal and meeting nights, leave a little extra time to make food preparation fun. Often you'll find that kids are more interested in eating foods that they had a hand in preparing.

By allowing them to participate, you not only encourage them to eat, but also teach them the joys of cooking. You'd be surprised how many young adults don't even know how to boil water because they were never shown cooking basics. And remember to be flexible: sometimes French toast or scrambled eggs for dinner is a great way to build their confidence and have fun cooking and eating together.

I hope these tips on how to select and prepare nutritious meals with a minimum of fuss and bother – time spent in the kitchen will detract from your family meals and meetings, so let's get some quick and easy meals on the table and let's go!

# Special Added Bonus Section on Manners

When our good friend Maralee McKee, Founder and Director of The Protocol School of Orlando, heard that I was writing a book about the importance of family meals and meetings, she got very excited and asked what I had included about table manners. When I told her that we really hadn't got into that, she graciously offered to give us a quickie primer on manners. Needless to say, we were delighted. This next section was written by Maralee, and you can contact her by email at ProtocolSchool@cfl.rr.com or see her Web site at www.protocolschool.com.

Thanks Maralee!

**FUN FACT**

# Impacting Dining Manners for the Family Table

Over the years etiquette has been taught much less -- first falling out of practice more and more since the late 1960's. Because of this, there's a general misconception that it's a set of passé "rules" known and used mostly by pretentious snobs, only in stuffy, formal occasions. Actually, etiquette is still relevant, and it always will be, because it continually evolves to meet the needs of the current generation.

Today's society has replaced many of the formal rules of the past with newer, easier guidelines for the whole family -- whether you're dining at a fast-food or a five-star restaurant.

By teaching your children table manners you're giving them a valuable tools... tools they can use to interact worry-free in public and private situations..  Children and teens appreciate that there's a "right," "best" way to accomplish a task and do not want to ever feel embarassed. When they're not worrying about the impression they're making they're free to enjoy themselves and to concentrate on the other person and the event.  The clear-cut boundaries of proper etiquette, gives them this freedom.

There's no better place to teach dining etiquette than around the family table -- where without fear of embarrassment your child can be taught the skills they need before they need them in public.

Remember, dining manners don't exist to complicate our mealtimes. Their purpose is to make our actions and reactions around the table more predictable and thus more easily managed.

Manners are the practical expression of our character. Because of this, dining manners should not be saved just on special occasions. These skills should be used every day so they become second nature, and so that our actions consistently demonstrate a level of self-confidence, respect for others, and appreciation for order and correctness.

**MEAL TIME**

# Setting the Table

For everyday meals at home setting the table correctly is straightforward and easy to master.

✔ First, place the plate in the center of each person's place setting.

✔ The items that go on the RIGHT of your plate all have five letters, the same number as in the word "Right." (glass, knife and spoon)

✔ Place the knife next to the plate with the glass directly above the knife. When a spoon is needed place it to the right of the knife.

✔ For children over the age of five, vegetables and starches (like mashed potatoes and corn) should be eaten with a fork. A spoon is not necessary at all meals.

✔ Some common foods you might eat with a spoon include: gelatin, applesauce, yogurt, cereal, ice cream, pudding and of course, soup.

✔ Although you have to play with the words a little, it will help your child remember which items go to the LEFT of their plate by changing the words to ones that have four letters. The items that go on the left are: fork, roll (bread of any type) and napkin. "Fork" and "roll" are fine because they both have four letters. To get "napkin" to fit remember that it's used to "wipe" your fingers and lips and you have another four-letter reminder.

✔ The napkin is placed to the left of the fork, not under it, because it is the first item used in the place setting. (Etiquette states that once a utensil is touched it should not touch the table again. Putting the napkin under the fork requires us to touch the fork to get to the napkin.)

✔ For special meals a napkin may be folded into fun shapes and placed directly on the plate.

# Coming to the Table

**TOGETHER**

✔ Remain standing until everyone comes to the table. Mom, as the hostess, should be the first to sit. After that, the other women or young ladies are seated. Then the men and boys may sit.

✔ To avoid bumping into one another, always enter and exit a chair the same way. As you pull the chair out, enter it from the chair's right. (Your left leg will be the first to come into contact with the chair.) Exit in the same direction you entered.

✔ If your family says "grace," do not touch anything on the table, put your napkin on your lap, or take a drink until it's finished. If a clergy member is present at the meal, he or she is usually offered the honor of praying. Other than that, any member of the family is free to offer the blessing. You may want to ask the person before coming to the table to avoid putting him or her on the spot.

✔ As a sign of appreciation for the hostess, once food is served, she is the first one to begin each course by picking up her fork and beginning to eat.

# Passing and Requesting Food

**MEAL TIME**

✔ For a family meal where everyone is seated around one table, all the food should be passed before anyone begins to eat.

✔ Help yourself to whatever dish is in front of you and then pass it to your right. All food should go around the table and end up back where it began.

✔ It's kind to hold the dish for the person on your right so it's easier for them to serve themselves.

✔ Pay attention to others. If you notice someone has eaten the item that was in the dish in front of you, offer them another serving.

✔ If an item has been passed around the table once, it no longer has to be passed to the right. Pass it in the shortest possible route.

✔ If everyone has had an opportunity to take a portion of each dish, and you see there's more left, it's correct to request a second helping. In fact, it's a compliment to the cook!

✔ Always pass the salt and pepper together, even if only one was requested. Do not hand it to the person next to you, instead each person should sit it down in front of the next person.

# Use Your Napkin Please

**MEAL TIME**

✔ The hostess will be the first to remove her napkin and place it on her lap to signal that the meal has begun. Everyone else should now put their napkin on their laps.

✔ Unfold your napkin once it's on your lap -- not in mid-air.

✔ Keep your napkin folded in half, with the fold facing your waist.

✔ Wipe your fingers and lips on the top portion of the fold. The bottom half, touching your clothes, is then kept as a barrier between the soiled portion and your clothes.

✔ Wipe your fingers often -- especially before passing anything.

✔ Wipe your lips each time before taking a drink to keep food particles and lipstick from forming a mark on the glass.

✔ If, for any reason, you leave the table, place your napkin on the seat of your chair and push your chair under the table. No one should be left looking at your dirty napkin while you're away from the table.

✔ To avoid getting the seats of the chair dirty, remember to place the clean side of the napkin against the cushion.

✔ To signal the end of the meal, the hostess will be the first to remove her napkin from her lap and place it to the left of her plate. Everyone else should now do the same.

# It's a Spoon, Not a Shovel

✔ Once a piece of silverware has been picked up, no part of it should touch the table again throughout the meal.

✔ Cut one bite of food at a time. This keeps food from becoming cold too quickly; it slows our eating down, and keeps our plates looking less messy.

**REMEMBER**

✔ Make sure to cut , not saw, your food -- cutting in one direction only.

✔ After cutting a bite, place your knife at an angle in the top right-hand corner of the plate.

✔ Do not hold your fork between bites. While chewing, talking or taking a drink, lay your fork down on the plate. If you picture the plate like a clock, the tines will face toward 10 o'clock. The handle will touch 4 o'clock.

✔ When you've completed a course place your knife and fork together in the same resting position as was used for the fork only in-between bites.

✔ To help keep the utensils from falling off when the plate is removed, make sure that the handles of the knife and fork don't stick off the plate more than one inch.

# "Excuse Me, Please!"

**EXAMPLE**

Dining mishaps are bound to happen. If you know how to handle them before they occur, you can minimize embarrassment when they do.

✔ If someone at the table burps, they should softly say, "Excuse me please." No one at the table should comment unless it's to say, "Of course" or to smile slightly as if to say, "I understand you didn't do it on purpose."

✔ Any bodily function other than a burp should be considered an "unmentionable." No comment by the offender or the other diners needs to be made. If you're more comfortable saying, "Please excuse me," no one else should say anything. With maturity your children will be able to refrain from laughter.

✔ If someone needs to use the bathroom, they should be taught to leave the table quietly by simply saying, "Excuse me." The exception would be at restaurant when children need to seek a parent's permission and have someone go with them for safety's sake.

✔ You can wipe your nose at the table if you happen to have a tissue with you. Never use your napkin. Because of the rude sounds blowing your nose makes, it should be done away from the table. Likewise, if you feel a coughing spell coming on, leave the table until it subsides.

✔ For a random cough or sneeze, cover your mouth with a tissue. If one's not available use your napkin, not your hand.

# Handling Dining Accidents, Without Embarrassment

**WARNING**

✔ If you drop a piece of silverware on the floor of the restaurant, simply ask the server to bring you another. There's no need to pick up the dropped piece unless someone might trip over it.

✔ In someone's home, pick up the dropped silverware and ask for a replacement.

✔ If your napkin falls off your lap, and you feel the floor is clean enough, simply pick it up and place it back on your lap.

✔ In a restaurant, immediately tell the wait staff if a spill occurs to prevent others from slipping. If a piece of food drops, alert the staff only if it poses a safety hazard.

✔ At someone's house, alert the hostess immediately of any spill and offer to help clean it. If a piece of food drops that doesn't pose a tripping risk and won't stain the carpet, just leave it until after the meal.

✔ If crumbs and small pieces of food fall off the plate and land around your place-setting, feel free to subtly place them back on the edge of your plate to avoid drawing attention to them when the plate is removed for the next course to be served.

✔ If you spill something on someone else, offer your apologies and some napkins -- but let the other person do all the wiping.

# Tips for Savvy Dining

**IDEA**

✔ Try a little of all the food offered to you, unless you know you're allergic.

✔ Take small bites, so you can join in the conversation at any moment.

✔ Wait until you've swallowed what's in your mouth before taking another bite or a drink.

✔ When drinking, look into not over the glass.

✔ Tear just one bite of your roll off at a time to eat and butter it. Butter it on your plate, not in midair.

✔ Remove bones, seeds, pits, gristle and other alien objects with your thumb and first finger. Place them on the side of your dinner plate. If available, it's nice to hide them under the parsley or other plate garnish.

✔ For every meal, thank your host or hostess and compliment him or her on the food served or the restaurant chosen.

✔ Keep purses, papers and all other items that don't pertain to eating off the table during the meal.

✔ Remember your table posture. Keep both feet flat on the floor, and hands in your lap when not being used for cutting or eating. Sit up straight, with your back against the back of the chair. Push your chair all the way in, leaving approximately the width of your hand between you and the table. (Sitting this close aids in keeping food that falls off your fork from falling onto you lap.)

✔ Always bring the food up to your lips rather then bending down to the food.

# Common Dining Errors to Avoid

✔ Don't talk about diets, food other than what's being served, or restaurants while dining.

✔ Avoid overloading your plate. Instead help yourself to seconds.

✔ Never take medicine, use a toothpick, apply makeup or lipstick, look into a mirror or touch your head or hair while at the table.

**WARNING**

✔ Don't push your plate away to signal your finished eating. Simply lay your knife and fork with the handles facing four o'clock.

✔ Don't gesture with a utensil in your hand.

✔ Don't mix food on your plate together.

✔ Don't blow on your food or beverage; simply wait a moment for them to cool.

✔ Don't dunk in public or add more than one bite worth of crackers to your soup at a time!

**TOGETHER**

# Have Fun With the "Rules"

To make learning etiquette fun and memorable my family plays "Pass the Pig" to remind us of and to reward good dining manners. The rules aren't set-in-stone so feel free to change them to suit your family needs.

**How to play:**

1. Purchase a whimsical wood or ceramic pig.
2. Place it in the center of the table.
3. Every time someone at the table is caught not using good dining etiquette the pig is passed to them and they receive a pig-scratch (a tally).
4. When the next person is caught not at their best the pig passes to them.
5. At the end of the meal the person who had the pig the fewest number of times wins.

The prize for the winner must be agreed on before the game begins but can change every week. Possible prizes include:

✔ Getting the largest serving of dessert
✔ Not having to help clean the table
✔ Being able to choose the menu for the next family meal
✔ Staying up for 30 minutes past bedtime
✔ Choosing the Table Time topic for the next family meeting
✔ The list can go on and on. Choose whatever will be a motivating prize for your family.

While there might appear to be a lot of dining 'rules' to remember they really are straightforward and easy to master. When put into practice these etiquette skills become a vehicle to deliver the valuable character traits of kindness, deference, patience and self-control in our everyday encounters with one another.

# Chapter Seventeen
## Help Is Available

## Call Your Parents

> "Everyone should be a grandparent before they're a parent." I don't know who first penned this genetically impossible advice, but they're right. We grandparents have much better hindsight than foresight, and, if we could do it over again, most of us would make some adjustments.
>
> Mike Bellah, in *A Grandparents Advice To Parents*

**QUOTES**

> One of the great gifts we have is our ability to influence young children. Removed from the power struggles of the immediate family a grandparent isn't likely to meet with as much resistance as a parent would in suggesting a child do some homework or set the table. It is one way grandparents help parents by reinforcing the values that parents want to instill.
>
> T. Berry Brazelton, in
> *Making it Work: A Grandparents Guide*

**TOGETHER**

As you're working your way through many of the thorny issues we've discussed in this book, never lose sight of the fact that you probably know some people all this stuff has happened to before: your parents, or your in-laws. There's nothing wrong with picking up the phone and asking for a little advice. It is true that you're faced with some parenting issues that your parents never had to deal with. But, as we've been discussing all along throughout this book, you can go a long way towards heading off most problems by giving your kids a basic grounding in values.

And whether you realize it or not – and I'm betting you realize it more every day as you get older – your parents are the people who imbedded you with the basic values that you try to live your life by on a day-to-day basis. So when it seems like the kids are going to drive you right up the wall, pick up the phone and call your parents. It might just be that they can shed a little light on the subject for you, and get you headed back on the correct parenting course.

# Talk to Your Spiritual Advisor

**QUOTES**

> "Apply your heart to instruction and your ears to words of knowledge."
>
> Proverbs 23:12

If you're not lucky enough to be able to draw on your parents or in-laws for advice (or even if you are and you still need more help) your spiritual advisor in the faith of your choice is usually a good resource. Talk to your priest, rabbi, imam, pastor (or whatever the head of your congregation is called). If they don't have an answer for you, they can almost certainly point you in the direction of an agency that can help you find the advice you seek.

If you'd like some non-denominational faith-based advice, you can always call the Covenant House Nineline at 800-999-9999. The people at Covenant House began their mission shepherding runaways in New York City, and have expanded nationwide to help families in trouble.

Here's how they word their open-handed invitation to use their advice line:

When you are upset, it's hard to think logically about what is best. That's why Nineline exists. They:

✔ Talk with you whether or not you tell us your name or where you are

✔ Listen to what's going on at home, help sort out the problem and think about who can help

✔ Help figure out how to talk with your child

✔ Find someone nearby to talk with

✔ And we don't judge - we just listen.

Covenant House

**REMEMBER**

# Local and Governmental Resources

"Life affords no greater responsibility, no greater privilege, than the raising of the next generation."
C. Everett Koop M.D, former U.S. Surgeon General

It really is comforting, when you actually look at the amount of support our local, sate and federal governments offers parents from all walks of life. There is an almost overwhelming amount of advice offered online for free, and almost all of the government Web sites offer advice on how to get help locally. It's kind of nice to see our tax dollars at work on something so important!

You can pick up any local phone book and look under Social Services, or the Department of Social Services and get some help and advice for free – it's important to remember that you're not alone in your parenting endeavor. You can always pick up the phone and call your parents, friends, your spiritual advisor, or the government for help.

# We Asked for a Lot of Help Along the Way... and We Got it!

Over the last four years, as Neal and I and our family worked out exactly what *Family Table Time* was, and what it meant to us, we were never shy about picking up the phone and asking someone for help on something. And here's what we have to say to all of those who helped us along the way:

*The Kimball family offers our sincere thanks for the support and guidance you have given us during the process of creating Family Table Time.*

*We all know that time is a gift. You have shared your gift of time and have brought Family Table Time to life.*

*Our passion has been ignited by your input, support and commitment. We are forever Grateful!*

*Your handprint has been permanently etched in Family Table Time. The Kimball Family*

Jill Kimball          Neal Kimball

Jimmy Kimball          Kyle Kimball

CAITLIN KIMBALL          Maggie Kimball

Finally, we'd like to thank you for picking up our book, and we'd like to offer all of you the sincerest best wishes and good luck when you're set to begin holding family meals and meetings in your house.

# Chapter Seventeen

# Appendix
## Extra Resource Guide

## Suggested Online Resource Guide

We'd like to share with you some Internet sites that we've found helpful along the way, and we hope that you find them helpful too. Remember, even if you don't have an Internet connection at home, your local library has Internet-capable computers available and the librarians there will help you get online.

Note: All of these sites were used in researching this book, and although we credited the authors whenever we quoted someone, I wanted to make sure we included them here as well. *Where the site description is listed in quotes that means that I used the site's own description.*

**Adolescence and Peer Pressure**
http://www.ianr.unl.edu/pubs/family/nf211.htm
This University of Nebraska site features a great article on peer pressure by Herbert G. Lingren, Family Scientist

**America's Promise**
http://www.americaspromise.com/
"America's Promise is a collaborative network that builds upon the collective power of communities and partners to help fulfill the Five Promises for every young person in America."

**American Association For Marriage and Therapy**

http://www.aamft.org/index_nm.asp

Advice on how to find a family therapist and related issues.

**Barna Research Online**

http://www.barna.org/

"Barna Research Group, Ltd. (BRG) is a full-service marketing research company located in Ventura, California. BRG has been providing information and analysis regarding cultural trends and the Christian Church since 1984."

**BC Parent Online**

http://www.bcparent.com/articles/Fall_2002/silent_witness.html

An article on bullying by *Cathleen Chance Vecchiato*, featuring information from Richard B.Goldblum, MD.

**The Changing American Family**

http://www.context.org/ICLIB/IC21/Fraser.htm

An informative piece on American families by Arvonne S. Fraser, Senior Fellow at the Humphrey Institute of Public Affairs, University of Minnesota.

**Children's Home Society of Washington**

http://www.chs-wa.org/1_about.htm

"Children's Home Society of Washington's Parent Information and Resource Center (PIRC) Online... parents, educators, and kids can find helpful tips, local community resources, and ideas for fun family activities."

**Christianity.com**

http://home.christianity.com/

Probably not to hard to figure out what this site is about either!

**Covenant House**

http://www.covenanthouse.org/nineline/care_fi_06.html

Help for at-risk kids and parents of at-risk kids.

**The Domestic Church**

http://www.stpatrickstlawrence.org/Documents/Family%20Ministry/THE%20DOMESTIC%20CHURCH.htm

An essay on the concept of the Domestic Church.

**Education World: The Educators Best Friend**

http://www.education-world.com

Resources for teachers (and why shouldn't parents use this also? I did!) on a broad variety of subjects.

**The Essence of Family**

http://www.context.org/ICLIB/IC21/Robin.htm

An interesting piece by Vicki Robin published in Context: A Quarterly of Humane Sustainable Culture.

**Family First**

www.familyfirst.net The mission of Family First is to strengthen the family by establishing family as a top priority in people's lives and by promoting principles for building marriages and raising children.

**Families First: Keys to Successful**
**Family Functioning: Communication**

http://www.ext.vt.edu/pubs/family/350-092/350-092.html

Some great papers by Rick Peterson, Extension Specialist and Assistant Professor, Department of Human Development, and Stephen Green, Graduate Student, Department of Human Development, Virginia Tech

**Family Communication and Family Meetings**

http://www.ext.nodak.edu/extpubs/yf/famsci/fs522w.htm

A great paper by Deb Gebeke, Family Science Specialist, Kim Bushaw, Parent Line Program Specialist of North Dakota State University

**Family Stress Test**

http://www.plainsense.com/Health/Stress/family.htm

This page is an online family stress test. Part of a larger site that "helps with everyday health questions that individuals may have by clarifying general definitions and helps to alert one if medical attention is necessary."

**Family Table Time**

http://www.familytabletime.com

I bet you can't guess what this site is about!

**Hazelden Center For Youth and Families**

http://www.hazelden.org/visit_us.dbm

"Hazelden is a non-profit organization providing high quality, affordable addiction treatment, education, publishing and research for more than 50 years."

**Helping Your Child through Early Adolescence**

http://www.ed.gov/pubs/parents/adolescence/index.html

Invaluable advice from the Department of Education on raising adolescents.

**Helpful Hints for Reducing Family Stress**

http://www.mental-health-matters.com/articles/article.php?artID=422

This page offers tips on reducing family stress, part of a larger site that cover mental health topics in general.

**Images Puppet Production**

http://www.imagepuppets.on.ca

Faith education for kids.

**International Association of Eating Disorder Profesionals**

http://www.iaedp.com

Where and how to get information and help on eating disorders.

**Journal of Psychology**

http://www.apa.org/journals/fam.html

Here's where you can find a pdf file of *A Review of 50 Years of Research on Naturally Occurring Family Routines and Rituals: Cause for Celebration?*, Barbara H. Fiese, Thomas J. Tomcho, Michael Douglas, Kimberly Josephs, Scott Poltrock, and Tim Baker; Syracuse University.

**Life Education Centres**

http://www.lifeeducationcentres.org.uk/factsheets.php

This U.K. based site offers a series of free Fact Sheets for Parents, specially designed to support drug prevention in homes.

**Metropolitan Family Services**

http://www.metrofamily.org/articleDetail.asp?objectID=1075

An article by Kathleen Sheridan on helping children who were teased or bullied.

**Marriage and Family Life Books**

http://www.ashburnumc.org/main/resources/books/books_family_life.htm

Suggested reading list from the United Methodist Church

**Making Lemonade**

http://www.makinglemonade.com

A whole network of great resources for single parents.

**Methods For Gaining Insight Into Ourselves**

http://mentalhelp.net/psyhelp/chap15

A psychological self help site; this particular page deals with self-awareness, but many topics are available on the home page, mentalhealth.com

**National Center on Addiction and Substance Abuse at Columbia University (CASA)**

http://www.casacolumbia.org/

"A unique think/action tank that engages all disciplines to study every form of substance abuse as it affects our society." The National Center on Addiction and Substance Abuse (CASA) at Columbia University launched Family Day as an annual event, which takes place on the fourth Monday of each September.

**National Mental Health and Education Center**

http://www.naspcenter.org/teachers/peer_ho.html

This site features a great piece by Carlen Henington, Ph.D. of Mississippi State University called Peer Relationships in Childhood.

**National Parent Information Network**

http://www.npin.org

You should see the suggested reading section of this site!

**National PTA**

http://www.pta.org

This site offers parenting information ranging far past the expected school issues.

**Nutrition Education Network**

http://cahenews.wsu.edu/RELEASES/2001/01048.htm

Quick nutrition tips for parents.

**Our Family Place**

http://www.ourfamilyplace.com

A great resource for family financial planning tips and information.

**Parents Helping Parents, Inc. The Family Resource Center**

http://www.php.com/

Different support groups for parents.

**Parenting is Preventing**

http://www.parentingisprevention.org

Tips on keeping teens off drugs, and info about parenting support groups.

**Parenting Resources for the 21st Century**

http://www.parentingresources.ncjrs.org

This is the grand-daddy of all government parenting Web sites, with information and links to any possible parenting subject. "This site, federally sponsored through the Coordinating Council on Juvenile Justice and Delinquency Prevention, strives to help families meet the formidable challenges of raising a child today..."

**Parents Talk**

http://www.parents-talk.com

Advice from leading child care experts like T. Berry Brazelton.

**Parents; The Anti-Drug**

http://www.theantidrug.com

A government-sponsored site just brimming with all sorts of information on how to fight substance abuse, with links to all sorts of parenting advice

**Parents.com**

http://www.parents.com

This is the online version of *Parents* magazine.

**Pastoral Counselors**

http://www.aapc.org/

"Professionally integrating psychotherapy and spirituality - The American Association of Pastoral Counselors (AAPC) represents and sets professional standards for over 3,000 Pastoral Counselors and 100 pastoral counseling centers in North America and around the world."

**Pathways**

http://www.cfsla.org

Formerly called Child and Family Services, this site offers family support services in a variety of languages. This is a California state-funded site.

**Population Resource Center**

http://www.prcdc.org/summaries/family/family.html

Census figures and statistics based articles about the changing nature of the American family.

**Praize.com**

http://www.praize.com/kidz/q&a/God.html

This particular page is about kids questions on God; part of a larger Christian community web site.

**Psychological Self-Help**

http://mentalhelp.net/psyhelp/author.htm

About the author, Dr.Clay Tucker-Ladd.

**Public Agenda**

http://www.publicagenda.org/

Public Agenda is a nonpartisan, nonprofit public opinion research and citizen education organization based in New York City. It was founded in 1975 by social scientist and author Daniel Yankelovich and former Secretary of State Cyrus Vance.

**Public And Private Families**

http://highered.mcgrawhill.com/sites/0072405449/student_view0/census_2000_updates.html

"This web page provides links to recent population data pertaining to the topics presented in *Public and Private Families: An Introduction*. Information from the United States and the rest of the world can be accessed."

**Search Institute**

http://www.search-institute.org/

"To provide leadership, knowledge, and resources to promote healthy children, youth, and communities."

**Setting Goals For More Effective Parenting**

http://workplaceblues.com/relationships/setting.asp

One of many pages of parenting advice on this site that offers a lot of good advice on juggling work and family responsibilities

**Something Fishy**

http://www.something-fishy.org/

This is a site with support and help for victims and families of victims of eating disorders.

**Southern Poverty Law Center**

http://www.splcenter.org/

"The Southern Poverty Law Center is a nonprofit organization that combats, hate, discrimination and intolerance through education and litigation."

**StepFamilies in Formation**

http://sfhelp.org/pop/f-roles.htm

"This is one of 600+ Web pages exploring factors that promote long-term re/marital and stepfamily success. Each page is part of a complex stepfamily mosaic, so the more you read, the more sense they'll all make." This is also the place to find great stuff by Peter Gerlach, MSW, who wrote *About Family Roles And Role Conflicts: Help Each Other Agree On Who's Responsible For What*, among many other helpful pieces.

**Stress Manager**

http://www.umich.edu/~fasap/stresstips/contents.html

Help with stress from the Faculty and Staff Assistance Program at the University of Michigan.

**Supporting Your Adolescent: Tips For Parents**
http://www.ncfy.com/supporti.htm
Yet another helpful government web site on parenting, with a great reading list.

**Teen Program.info**
http://www.teenprogram.info/schools/view/429
"Watchdog" for troubled teen programs.

**The Right Question**
http://www.rightquestion.org
A nonprofit organization that helps parents get more involved in their children's education.

**The Successful Parent**
http://www.thesuccessfulparent.com
This is a parenting web site with info on child and adolescent development, parenting styles and approaches, and skill building for dealing with your specific parenting problems.

**The Truth About Drugs**
http://www.globalchange.com/drugs/TAD-Intro.htm
Dr. Patrick Dixon's informative substance abuse site.

**TV Parental Guidelines**
http://www.tvguidelines.org/
Advice on how to use your V-chip and the TV guidelines system.

**Web MD**
http://my.webmd.com
Practical everyday medical advice.

# Notes

# Notes